From:
Carole B. (signature)

Sherman's Other War

To: Alister —
Eileen —
Kirsty —
Michael &
Alexander

Jan. 12, 2000

Enjoy —
Dr. John F. Marszalek
was nominated for
the Pulitzer Prize several
years ago. A M.S.U.
History Professor!!

William Tecumseh Sherman, ca. 1870s.
Courtesy of the Library of Congress

JOHN F. MARSZALEK

Sherman's Other War

The General and the Civil War Press

THE KENT STATE UNIVERSITY PRESS
Kent, Ohio, and London

© 1981, 1999 by John F. Marszalek
All rights reserved
Library of Congress Catalog Card Number 98-13764
ISBN 0-87338-619-1 (pbk.)
Manufactured in the United States of America

Revised edition

First edition published by Memphis State University Press, 1981.

05 04 03 02 01 00 99   5 4 3 2 1

Library of Congress Cataloging-in-Publication Data

Marszalek, John F., 1939–
    Sherman's other war : the general and the Civil War press / John F. Marszalek. — Rev. ed.
      p. cm.
    Includes bibliographical references and index.
    ISBN 0-87338-619-1 (alk. paper)
    1. United States—History—Civil War, 1861–1865—Journalists. 2. Sherman, William T. (William Tecumseh), 1820–1891—Relations with journalists. 3. Freedom of the press—United States—History—19th century. 4. Journalists—United States—History—19th century.
I. Title.
E609.M37   1998
973.7'8—dc21   98-13764

British Library Cataloging-in-Publication data are available.

For My Parents

Freedom of speech and freedom of the Press, precious relics of former history, must not be construed too largely.
—General William T. Sherman, 27 October 1863

[Y]ou are regarded the enemy of our set, and we must in self-defense write you down.
—Reporter Thomas W. Knox, February 1863

Contents

PREFACE	ix
ACKNOWLEDGMENTS	xiii
1 THE FIRST AMENDMENT IN WAR	3
2 THE ANTAGONISTS	37
3 "THE INSANE GENERAL"	63
4 THE CZAR OF MEMPHIS	108
5 THE PRESS ON TRIAL	131
6 THE MARCH MINUS REPORTERS	168
7 SHERMAN STUMBLES	197
CONCLUSION	224
BIBLIOGRAPHICAL NOTE	229
INDEX	245

Preface

It has been over fifteen years since the first edition of this book appeared. At that time, in 1981, the nation was still grappling with the immediate implications of the Vietnam War and the trauma of the resignation of President Richard M. Nixon. Print and television media had played an important role in both cataclysmic events; a significant number of Americans blamed or credited correspondents with getting the nation out of the Asian War or losing it, unfairly bringing down a president or ridding the nation of a menace to the constitution.

A book detailing the anti-press activities of a major American military leader in the nineteenth century, therefore, seemed timely in those turbulent days. William T. Sherman's battle with Civil War reporters resonated at a time when Richard Nixon and his vice president, Spiro T. Agnew, railed against the media, and military figures, both famous and in the trenches, blamed the press for the loss in Vietnam.

As was the case in the 1970s, the political-military-media battle during the Civil War seemed to focus on the First Amendment of the United States Constitution. What did the Founding Fathers mean when they guaranteed freedom of the press in the Bill of Rights? Were press rights the same in wartime as they were in peace? How far could leading politicians and military leaders go in defending their positions on the issue? Where did defense of the constitution or of national security begin and end?

In the years since 1981, the issue of the media in time of war has been argued and reargued several times. President Ronald Reagan invaded Grenada in 1983 and launched air strikes against Libya in 1985. President George Bush sent troops into Panama in 1989, the Persian Gulf in 1991, and Somalia in 1992. President William Clinton maintained troops in Somalia and placed military units in Haiti and Bosnia. In all these cases there was no declaration of war, but the American military faced combat anyway and worked to control reporters, actually to eliminate them from the battlefield. Meanwhile, the federal courts dealt with suits that unsuccessfully sought judicial resolution of the problem.

The actions of these late-twentieth-century presidents, therefore, have shown that the issue of press freedom within the context of the protection of national security has not yet been resolved. If anything, the issue has become even more problematic than before. The national government has asserted and assumed definitive control over the media in several modern wartime situations, determining that it has the power and authority to exclude reporters completely and give the American public its own perception of events. The military has clearly gained the upper hand over correspondents on the battlefield.

Once again, therefore, and even more than was the case in 1981, a book that discusses the anti-press activities of a leading Civil War general has lessons for modern times. William T. Sherman's war against reporters and their battle with him are concrete demonstrations of the issues that continue to dog modern Americans at war, even to the end of the twentieth century.

The central figure of this study, William T. Sherman, spent a great deal of time and energy pondering and acting on this question. His anti-press views stand out more than anyone else's in American military history because of his conclusion that there was a direct relationship between press censorship and military victory. He was never satisfied with the disjointed government censorship activity during the Civil War, so he diligently and consistently tried to implement his own more severe anti-press ideas. He fought a war with newspaper reporters at the same time he was fighting the Confederacy. His actions provide insight into the motives and thoughts of similar anti-press public figures at other times in American history.

Civil War newspapers and their correspondents were equally determined to protect what they considered to be their constitutional guarantees. They battled government restrictions and those military men who tried to enforce them. Since Sherman's anti-press activities were so blatant, he was a constant target of intense newspaper counterfire. As a result, two determined forces (Sherman and the press) vied for the victory each saw as central to its cause's success. Their war within a war exemplified the difficulties inherent in the universal problem of freedom of the press within a democracy at war.

It might seem that the Sherman-press Civil War battle was the result of a difference in constitutional interpretation. Sherman believed that the press should have no rights during war. Reporters, on the other hand, maintained that their rights were no different in war than they were in peace. Winning the war took precedence over the Bill of Rights, said Sherman; maintain the Bill of Rights over and above everything else, said the newspapers. The inevitability of conflict was obvious, given these two views.

Actually, as this book will attempt to show, neither Sherman nor the Civil War correspondents developed a consistent constitutional philosophy. Their battle was more a personal conflict than a constitutional debate, and, for this reason, it has historical relevance. Given the fact that, historically, press control in wartime has been less a constitutional than an ad hoc reaction to the immediate circumstances, and given the fact that such is still the situation, a study of American history's leading anti-press military man continues to have obvious significance for the present and the future.

Acknowledgments

This book would not have been possible without the support of many people at all stages of its composition. Professor Vincent P. DeSantis of the University of Notre Dame guided me in my early researches into this topic, and he has continued to encourage me in the years since. The late Professor David J. Gorman of Canisius College first introduced me to the joys of history, then became a friend who encouraged and supported me thereafter.

Personnel at numerous libraries, repositories, and archives made their resources available and offered generous help besides. These included: Manuscript Division of the Library of Congress; Cincinnati Historical Society; Kentucky Room of the Louisville Free Public Library; Special Collections, Butler Library, Columbia University; Chicago Historical Society; Ohio Historical Society; Henry E. Huntington Library; the National Archives and Records Service, Washington; Canisius College Library; University of Notre Dame Memorial Library; Buffalo and Erie County Public Library; Gannon College Library; Erie (Pa.) Public Library; Mitchell Memorial Library, Mississippi State University; and, most important of all, the University of Notre Dame Archives, particularly its former director, the late T. T. McAvoy, C. S. C.

Many individuals besides those already mentioned were instrumental in the completion of this work: President James D. McComas, Dean Edward McGlone, Associate Dean Charles Lowery, and History

Department Head William E. Parish, all of Mississippi State University, arranged for financial support; James F. Sefcik, Supervisor of Museum Operations, State Museum, Albany, New York; Professors Howard Ball and William E. Parrish of Mississippi State University and Professor James Smart of Keene State College, New Hampshire, all read the manuscript and offered important suggestions; Gannon College Student Assistant Patrick Casey and Mississippi State University Student Assistants Helen Thompson and Charles Morris provided essential research and typing help; Professor John Fleming of the Gannon College Psychology Department offered valuable advice concerning Sherman's mental health; Professor Jimmy G. Shoalmire, former head of Special Collections, Mitchell Memorial Library, Mississippi State University, established contact for me with Defense Department and U.S. Army officials leading to information on contemporary military views on the media; Mr. and Mrs. Joseph Sommers of Crofton, Maryland, Mr. and Mrs. Lawrence Held, now of San Francisco, and Professor Paul Simon of Xavier University, Cincinnati, Ohio, provided hospitality and patient ears during research trips; Sister Rosalie Marszalek, G. N. S. H., of Buffalo, New York, typed goodly sections of the first draft, while Rosemary Stewart of Erie, Pennsylvania, did her usual excellent work in typing an intermediate draft; my wife, Jeanne Kozmer Marszalek, spent long hours proofreading and typing and offered the encouragement and, when necessary, the solace without which this work would never have been completed. Our three sons, John, Chris, and Jamie, helped by trying to keep quiet during writing sessions.

Acknowledgments

Parts of this book, in different form, have previously appeared in historical journals: *Civil War Times Illustrated, Military Law Review,* and *Northwest Ohio Quarterly.* The editors of these journals have graciously given their permission to use this material.

Most of all, I want to thank the persons to whom this book is dedicated. My mother and my late father, Mr. and Mrs. John F. Marszalek, Sr., of Buffalo, New York, made many sacrifices to allow me, my brother, and my sisters to gain the formal education circumstances kept from them. These few words are hardly repayment in kind because their example, their encouragement, and their love has been so important through the years.

Addendum to Acknowledgments

Several persons were particularly helpful in the preparation of this book for publication as a paperback. John T. Hubbell, the director of the Kent State University Press, suggested the project and patiently waited for the revised manuscript. Michael B. Ballard, Charles D. Lowery, and William E. Parrish, all of Mississippi State University, offered their usual cogent criticisms. Susan Hall and Jackie Cloutman of the Interlibrary Loan Department, Mitchell Memorial Library, Mississippi State University, efficiently tracked down my many requests. Bridgette Neely, my student-assistant, deciphered my constant changes on the word-processed text and bibliography and somehow made sense of it all.

Sherman's Other War

I

The First Amendment in War

WILLIAM T. SHERMAN threatened to hang several reporters. He banished a number from his army. He even court-martialled one correspondent. On numerous occasions, newspapermen wrote that Sherman was insane. Throughout the Civil War, this famous general battled the press in a conflict that in intensity rivaled the fighting between Union and Confederate soldiers. The controversy focused on one issue: the meaning of the term "freedom of the press."

Throughout American history, First Amendment guarantees have been interpreted differently, and the question of press freedoms especially has been hotly debated. American newspapers, as agencies of information as well as opinion and argumentation, have frequently come under attack, and the meaning of the constitutional guarantee has been questioned. What responsibilities accompany a newspaper's privileges? How can the right of the American people to a free press (i.e., the right to know and express opinions) be protected in light of other Bill of Rights guarantees and the legitimate need for the American government, under certain circumstances, to maintain security?

During wartime, the problem of a free press and the government's need to maintain secrecy becomes more crucial. In a democracy the successful prosecution of a war is impossible without popular support. Yet, what if the press, by fulfilling the vital function of informing the people and rallying them behind the war effort, also provides information that harms the army on the battlefield? Or what if press criticism turns the populace against the war to the detriment of the national interest? More to the point, who is to decide what constitutes legitimate news and what is printed intelligence, and how is such a determination to be enforced? Is any censorship a violation of the First Amendment, and, if so, what then can be done to prevent valuable information from reaching the enemy?

These questions and many like them have been and continue to be matters of concern. Beginning with World War I, the First Amendment has been the subject of continued debate, yet this debate has not produced definitive answers. Rather, First Amendment guarantees have continued to provoke controversy. The matter of press freedoms during wartime has received even less consideration and certainly no definitive statement. The First Amendment in battle has been an important but little studied question.

In the early history of the United States, the nation experienced the repressive Alien and Sedition

Acts, which were a direct assault on freedom of expression. Fortunately, these laws were allowed to lapse in the early years of the nineteenth century, and they came to be viewed as exceptions to the more general climate of freedom. Americans prided themselves on their right to speak their minds and publish their opinions on contemporary issues without fear of official reprisals. (Editors of antislavery newspapers disagreed, but they were ignored.)

The United States experienced several wars during the nineteenth century, but, with the exception of the Civil War, the interpretation of the Bill of Rights during wartime was not an important issue. Indeed, the Supreme Court did not even consider a wartime freedom of expression case until the post-World War I period. Even then, the decisions dealt exclusively with the home front. *Schenck* v. *U.S.*,[1] *Abrams* v. *U.S.*,[2] *Pierce* v. *U.S.*[3] and *U.S.* ex rel *Milwaukee Democrat Publishing Company* v. *Burleson*[4] considered various First Amendment controversies and concluded that the government had the authority to limit expression that was found to be detrimental to the war effort. All these decisions focused on home-front opposition to the war effort, so the rights of reporters in the war zone to publish battlefield information was not clarified.

In the years since World War I, the Supreme Court has issued several significant First Amendment decisions, but only a couple have involved the matter of reporters in battle zones. Still, most of the decisions touch on this question. In the peacetime *Near* v. *Minnesota* decision, the Supreme Court rejected the concept of prior restraint; a newspaper, the Court ruled, could not be prevented from publishing any news story.[5] Forty-five years later, in *Nebraska Press Association* v. *Stuart*, the Court once more reaffirmed this anti–prior restraint concept.[6]

These two decisions, as important as they are, were made in peacetime situations concerning peacetime issues. Prior restraint in time of war remained unsettled. In 1971, however, this issue came before the Supreme Court for the first time. In the so-called Pentagon Papers case, government authorities asked the Court to prevent further publication of certain classified documents because of an alleged "grave and irreparable danger to national security" during the undeclared Vietnam War.[7] For the first time in American history, the federal government attempted to enforce prior restraint against newspapers, and this occurred during a time when the nation was at war.

The Court ruled in the amazingly quick time of two weeks; a short unsigned per curiam order rejected the government's attempt at restraint. In separate opinions, the justices said that the government had not conclusively proven the need for prior restraint; the newspapers in question were, therefore, not prevented from publishing the documents. But the issue was hardly settled conclusively. Justice William Brennan, of the majority, cited *Near* v. *Minnesota* in arguing that prior restraint was permissible only in time of war. William O. Douglas, another majority justice, saw no legal basis for prior restraint at any time, and he too cited the *Near* case. Justice Harry Blackmun, one of the dissenting minority, castigated the undue haste of the decision and then expressed a key point. "What is needed here," he said, "is a weighing upon properly developed standards of the broad right of the press to print and of the very narrow right of the Government to overturn."[8]

In short, the Pentagon Papers case established no solid precedent because it dealt only with the issue directly at hand, and at the time restraints were so great that a majority opinion could not be formulated. It seems clear, however, that the newspapers in question would have been enjoined from printing the Pentagon Papers if the government had been able to prove that such publication was an irreparable threat to national security.

In 1979 the issue surfaced again and seemed well suited for the needed precedent. A freelance writer, a one-time physics student, wrote an article for *The Progressive* magazine in Wisconsin on how to make a hydrogen bomb. He used information from encyclopedias and other public sources. The magazine's editors sent the article to the Department of Energy for evaluation, and the government agency immediately ruled that material in the article violated the Atomic Energy Act of 1954. The Energy Department volunteered, nonetheless, to work with the author to eliminate the allegedly classified material so that the article might yet be published. *The Progressive* editor, Erwin Knoll, refused and told the Energy Department to get a temporary restraining order or the magazine would publish the article as it was.

The Department of Energy went to the Federal Court for the Western District of Wisconsin, and Judge Robert Warren issued a preliminary injunction forbidding the publication of the article. The judge admitted that his order "would constitute the first instance of prior restraint against a publication in this fashion in the history of this country." Yet, he issued the temporary injunction, he said, because "publication of the technical information on the hydrogen bomb contained in the article is analogous to publication of troop movements or locations in time of war and falls within the extremely narrow exception to the rule against prior restraint" contained in *Near* v. *Minnesota* and in the Pentagon Papers case.[9]

The Progressive insisted it was a defender of the First Amendment, but the major media did not agree. Fearing that this case might result in a decision definitively establishing prior restraint, mainline newspapers and magazines castigated *The Progressive* for its recklessness. The *Washington Post*, which had itself played a major role in the Pentagon Papers case, printed a scathing editorial against the Wisconsin publication, while the *Saturday Review* said that "publishing the piece would be a crime against humanity." Undeterred that both the government and its press compatriots were in opposition, *The Progressive* argued in Federal Court against a permanent injunction. It said that the American public had a right to know all information, even that of a "dangerous" nature. The judge was not convinced, but he still hesitated to make his preliminary injunction permanent. He unsuccessfully suggested that the two parties mediate their differences. That failing, he issued a permanent injunction against *The Progressive*, prohibiting it from publishing the article.

The Progressive and the American Civil Liberties Union immediately appealed the decision to the Seventh Circuit Court of Appeals, arguing that the lower court had not met the judicial criteria of showing that publication of the hydrogen-bomb article would result in "immediate, grave, and irreparable damage" to national security. Keeping the magazine from publishing the article, i.e., prior restraint, "would not prevent the risk of nuclear destruction. That risk already exists."

Meanwhile, a computer programmer in California wrote a letter to U.S. senator Charles Percy in which he discussed the mechanism of a hydrogen bomb. The government immediately classified the letter, but it began appearing in minor newspapers anyway. Then a judge ordered the University of California at Berkeley newspaper not to follow the lead of these other papers, prohibiting it from publishing the letter. A small newspaper in Wisconsin, *The Madison Press Connection,* ignored this injunction and issued a special edition containing the letter. The government, therefore, dropped its case against *The Progressive,* and the Seventh Circuit Court of Appeals dismissed it. When *The Progressive* article became public, it was seen to contain information very much like that found in the *Encyclopedia Americana* article on the hydrogen bomb written by Edward Teller, the father of the thermonuclear device.

Obviously, the publication of this article did not prove as dangerous to national security as the government had claimed it would. It caused no nuclear proliferation. The case remained unsettled, however. Another justice, in another such case, might very well order prior restraint as Judge Warren had, and this order might stand. As a modern scholar phrased it, if a judge ever did that, "a large exception will have been gouged out of the First Amendment."[10]

A more recent court case, more directly concerned with the role of the press in wartime, was The Nation Magazine v. *United States Department of Defense* (1991).[11] Eight days into the Persian Gulf War, nine publications, five newsmen, a news agency, and a radio network asked the U.S. District Court for the Southern District of New York to stop the Defense Department from using prior restraint and a variety of other restrictions to prevent the press from covering the war. The plaintiffs argued that the government was acting not for reasons of national security but "to deter independent inquiry by the press, and to control and manipulate information available to the American public with respect to United States military activity."

Significantly, as in the *Progressive* case, the major media did not join its smaller brethren in making this argument. The major newspapers and the television networks protested the exclusionary tactics of the military, but they worried about going to court while the nation was at war. If the press lost this case, one that they considered weak, they believed that the First Amendment would be dealt a severe blow.

As a federal judge had done in a similar case in 1984 when the United States had invaded Grenada (*Flynt* v. *Weinberger* [1984])[12] the judge in the *Nation* case ruled that the suit against press restrictions was "moot" because the government had lifted restrictions, and the war was over anyway. Both judicial actions seemed to say that the press had a right to cover the American military in war but only in the context of the military's need for its safety. Every instance, these cases indicated, would have to be handled on an individual basis.

In *JB Pictures, Inc.* v. *Department of Defense* (1991),[13] however, a federal district judge decided and the U.S. Court of Appeals for the District of Columbia agreed that the military had the right to exclude the press and the public from a military installation, in this case Dover Air Force Base, where the bodies of servicemen and women killed in the Persian Gulf arrived home. A number of news organizations, veterans' groups, and the American Civil Liberties Union had hoped for an injunction against government exclusion, but the courts ruled that the press and the public in general had no *right* of access to military installations, especially in time of war. Unsaid but worrisome was whether a military installation might some day be judicially defined as the battlefield itself, and the press thereby legally excluded at the behest of political or military authorities.[14]

So, despite the First Amendment decisions since 1919, despite the implications of the prior restraint cases, the Supreme Court has not conclusively dealt with the matter of press rights in wartime. No case, for example, has specifically considered the extent of reporters' rights to gather and publish news in a combat zone or the permissible extent of press criticism of the war effort. "Historically," as a recent commentator has noted, "the Court has been reluctant to interfere with the operation of the military."[15] Yet, it is clear that the Court believes that, in war, First Amendment rights can be and are restricted in a manner not permitted in peacetime.

When the Civil War began, even this limited First Amendment judicial doctrine was not available; it was only during this war, indeed, that constitutional interpretation first shifted from concern over property rights to the area of individual rights. Concern over the right of habeas corpus, freedom of expression, right of trial, and so forth supplanted debate concerning the power of state and federal governments over commerce and contracts. The basic issue involved the viability of the Constitution in time of war, something constitutional historian Harold M. Hyman has referred to as the question whether the Constitution was "adequate" or "inadequate" for the prosecution of the war.[16]

The Civil War generation was divided over the Constitution's role in the war. Those who opposed the Lincoln administration, like the conservative Democrats, held that, even in wartime, the Constitution had to be strictly interpreted. As a Kentucky jurist wrote in 1861, "There is not, there can never be, in this country, a law of war different from the constitutional law of the land." Therefore, this view held, most of Lincoln's actions were unconstitutional, null, and void. Another group, persons like Radical Republicans Thaddeus Stevens and Charles Sumner, held that the Constitution was invalid during a war crisis. "War," Sumner thundered, "cannot be conducted *in vinculis*." The Constitution placed the government in chains; the government could not successfully fight the war in such a condition; therefore, the Constitution should be ignored for the duration of the war. A third view, that espoused by Lincoln, held that the Constitution remained in effect during war, and its extraordinary powers allowed the government to carry on the war effectively. Lincoln's position won out over the other views and the war was fought with the Constitution stretched but unimpaired. The postwar *Ex Parte Milligan* Supreme Court decision vindicated this view, and later American administrations took the same position in prosecuting twentieth century wars.[17]

The Civil War's First Amendment debate is part of these more general constitutional questions. Should the press in wartime retain all the Bill of Rights protections it had at any other time? Or should the First Amendment be eliminated for the duration of the crisis? Or should newspaper rights be regulated within the parameters of the First Amendment? Like the more general constitutional issues, the First Amendment debate was intense, and constitutional regulation won out over strict maintenance or total rejection of press rights. As a leading scholar of Civil War press restrictions has pointed out, "No true newspaper censorship existed during the war." The word censorship, for example, does not even appear in the index to the *Congressional Globe* or to the *Official Records*. Significantly, the major Civil War laws prohibiting disloyalty, the Conscription Act and the Treason Act, said nothing about newspapers.[18]

Still, the government did try to find an effective way to control newsmen. The absence of total censorship was less the result of a lack of desire and more the result of the character of the war, the want of previous experience—constitutional and practical—and the growing power of the newspapers. The government did not know how to act effectively in a situation where reporters easily infiltrated army camps or the neighboring populace to gain the story that the public wanted to read. Despite the government uncertainty, however, several kinds of regulation were tried.

The major way the government tried to control the press was by establishing telegraphic censorship. As early as 19 April 1861 Secretary of War Simon Cameron seized the telegraph lines outside Baltimore, Maryland, in order to isolate the anti-Union demonstrations there. Soon after, telegraph lines to and from Washington were put under government control and, over a period of time, censorship responsibility moved from the Treasury to the State to the War Departments. Telegraph censorship continued throughout the war, and its effectiveness varied with the quality of the censor as much as with anything else. In most instances, the censor proved unequal to the task, and reporters' complaints were frequent and vociferous. Often too, stories were transmitted despite the censor.[19]

When reporters had a particular problem with a telegraphic censor, they simply hand carried the offending story to the paper, or more often, sent it through the United States mail. Early in the war it became obvious that the mail could prove to be a

First Amendment in War 15

major loophole in any censorship program, so the government moved to plug it. On 16 August 1861 a New York grand jury was considering whether to indict certain local papers for allegedly treasonable utterances. No indictment was handed down, but the U.S. Postmaster General Montgomery Blair still took the occasion as justification for refusing to allow these newspapers to use the mail services. On 24 March 1862 he went further and ordered postmasters all over the country to notify the newspapers in their communities that, under penalty of exclusion from the mail, they were not to publish anything which had been excluded from the telegraph. These orders so upset the House of Representatives that its Judiciary Committee asked Blair what his authority for such action was. Blair replied that he had acted because the exigencies of war forced him to; in peacetime he certainly would not have issued any such order. The committee accepted this reasoning, agreeing that in the absence of congressional action the postmaster general had the duty to act. Throughout the war, then, the government tried to control reporters and newspapers by using the leverage it had in the mail service. Like the telegraph censorship, mail restrictions were not completely effective; reporters' stories got through and papers with contraband material were still usually delivered.[20]

Another method to try to control the nation's press was what would later be called voluntary censorship. In early July 1861 General Winfield Scott ordered that material he had not authorized could not be retransmitted over the telegraph. Reporters protested so vociferously that he met with them and they hammered out an agreement which allowed reporters to send stories about completed battles but prohibited them from mentioning any specific information about troop movements or soldier mutinies. The agreement quickly broke down. On 2 August 1861 General George B. McClellan's so-called Gentlemen's Agreement, the most famous such truce, was completed. Reporters promised not to send anything that would be of aid and comfort to the enemy, while the government promised to provide necessary press facilities and allow the transmission of stories over the telegraph. Such an agreement, it was hoped, would eliminate the need for censorship. In the first and second world wars, a similar voluntary censorship worked, but during the Civil War, it proved to be unsuccessful. Soon after the agreement, the government issued a sweeping regulation against the press, and newsmen similarly published information in violation of the agreement. Still, such a modus vivendi was often worked out between individual reporters and generals. Sometimes it worked, and other times it failed. The circumstances and the individuals involved determined success or failure.[21]

By far the most ominous government attempt at press control was the August 1861 resuscitation of a fifty-five-year-old law. In 1806 Congress had passed a code of laws governing the American military. The Fifty-Seventh Article of War, which was part of this law, stated that anyone "convicted of holding correspondence with or giving intelligence to the enemy either directly or indirectly shall suffer death or such other punishment as shall be ordered by the sentence of a court martial." In 1861 Simon Cameron, with Lincoln's signed approval, issued General Orders No. 67 stating that "all correspondence and communication, verbally, or by writing, printing, or telegraphing," about military operations without the approval of the commanding general would be considered a violation of the Fifty-Seventh Article of War. Reporters were thus subject to the death penalty for publishing stories that a court-martial board might find helped the enemy.[22] Fortunately, this regulation was almost universally ignored, or the press might well have been effectively destroyed. Only William T. Sherman of all the Civil War generals tried to use this regulation against a reporter.

Another method the government used against the nation's press was suppression of specific newspapers and incarceration of recalcitrant press personnel. During the course of the war, some ninety-two newspapers were subjected to some form of restriction, while forty-six others were attacked by mobs, often times soldiers on leave. The most famous cases of newspaper suppression were General Ambrose Burnside's action against the *Chicago Times* and General John A. Dix's action against the *New York World* and the *New York Journal of Commerce*. In both instances, the papers were quickly restored to publication, and their antiwar activities were little dampened. Still, fear of similar action kept the press wary and perhaps inhibited any movement toward complete license.[23]

Sometimes government regulations, in addition to being ineffective, were also ludicrous. In May 1864 the War Department directed reporters to register in person at the headquarters of the Army of the Potomac. Such registration would provide correspondents with passes granting permission to be in the area. However, no reporter could go to the headquarters without first having a pass. Press protest over this obvious contradiction proved futile until the dilemma was taken to Abraham Lincoln. The chief executive issued some presidential passes and temporarily broke the impasse. When Richmond, fell, however, Secretary of War Edward Stanton again ordered reporters to stay away.[24]

Early in the war, reporters learned an important lesson. Despite official government pronouncements, the commander in the field had the final say. If he wanted to enforce a particular decree, it would be enforced. If he did not care, the decree would be ignored no matter what anyone in the government hierarchy might say. The *New York Tribune* protested the inequity of this situation, which, it said, allowed "the parasites and toadies of Commanding Generals . . . as a favor to accompany them as chroniclers," while good reporters were kept out. Field commanders only enforced government regulations after they had interpreted them, and this gave them ultimate power. As a leading constitutional historian has pointed out, so long as generals in the field adhered to civilian direction in most matters and kept on winning, these military men were left pretty much alone. "Congress, courts, and President understood the wartime reality."[25]

The Civil War, then, was much like other American wars in the area of military-press relations. Correspondents attempted to get as close to the action as possible to report all they thought was newsworthy. Government officials and military men, on the other hand, tried to limit the information presented in newspapers. Officers in the field had practical ultimate authority.

Some form of censorship has existed in every American war since the Civil War, with the methods generally similar to those of 1861-1865. The Spanish-American War saw telegraph and cable censorship; World War I witnessed the promulgation of specific rules of conduct for reporters in the war zone; and World War II saw the development of a voluntary censorship system under a highly organized federal press bureaucracy. In each of these cases, there was little difficulty because of the common agreement on war objectives and the cooperation of reporters and government officials.[26]

With the coming of the undeclared Korean and Vietnam wars, all this changed. In the earlier declared wars, the predominant attitude was one of unity and purpose on war aims and objectives. There was, therefore, general consensus among the government, the people, and newsmen. Control of the flow of information was less difficult and censorship less onerous. During World War II, for example, Franklin D. Roosevelt exemplified this basic agreement when he said: "All Americans abhor censorship, just as they abhor war. But the experiences of this and other nations has demonstrated that some degree of censorship is essential in war time." The absence of animosity in this statement is obvious. During the Vietnam War, on the other hand, there was no general consensus on the conflict, and the government, the public, and the press developed an adversarial relationship. An Assistant Secretary of Defense for Public Affairs told reporters: "Look, if you think any American official is going to tell the truth then you're stupid." "American correspondents," a reporter remembered being told, "had a patriotic duty to disseminate only information that made the United States look good." News stories, after all, "were part of the weaponry."[27] The mutual distrust evidenced by this statement is clear. As in the Civil War, the lack of agreement during Korea and Vietnam made government-press relations a very difficult problem.

Technology threw new complications into the already confrontational press-military relations of the Vietnam War. Television reporters were a new breed, presenting problems for the military that the newsprint reporters never had or never could have. Instead of dealing with correspondents carrying notebooks and pencils or even a still or motion-picture camera, the military now saw on their battlefields reporters carrying lightweight cameras which could transmit pictures to American television sets instantaneously. Despite the fact that there was actually very little portrayal of the horror of war and that most television reporters reflected the government and the military viewpoint, Americans did see war in a firsthand manner never experienced before.[28]

The military response to both the old and the technologically new reporters was, at first, officially benign. What censorship existed was voluntary. Early in the Vietnam War the military established guidelines, but they were less onerous than those which had existed during World War II. Reporters were free to go wherever they wished, hopping rides on military helicopters or trucks and observing operations. Some two thousand reporters covered the Vietnam War, and there were only six instances of reporter activity that the military thought violated security. But there was a propensity on the part of the press to feature the sensational and ignore the commonplace, and military men were suspicious of the journalists' presence.

Consequently, serious animosity developed quickly. Reporters grew angry at what they believed was a conscious military effort to manipulate them in the daily briefings, what came to be called the "Five o'clock Follies," while military men felt betrayed when reporters criticized them and their activities. As the war grew militarily worse and the press criticism mounted, military animosity toward reporters increased. Quickly, the press reports, not the floundering war, became, in the military mind, the reason for the growth of the anti-war movements. When the war ended unsuccessfully, military men were convinced that the press had done them in. As late as 1995, 64 percent of active duty army officers surveyed in a poll blamed the media for the American loss in the Vietnam War.[29]

During the Vietnam War, soldiers, sailors, and marines decided that any future wars had to be, unlike Vietnam, short and immediately successful and that the press had to be controlled from the earliest days of action. Limit and control the media at the beginning, the military came to believe, and determine what information the public receives. Keep the pressure on until some other event captures the media's short attention.[30]

In the early 1980s, American political and military leadership watched with more than passing interest how the British controlled the press during the Falkland Islands War. Realizing the importance of public opinion in a democracy, British officials worked hard to make sure that the British public saw and read only that which maintained the people's support of the war. The British made sure that television images were positive, that only those reporters were allowed into the theater of war who could be trusted to present the military view, and that those correspondents who would not be cooperative were excluded. Finally, the British maintained a firm censorship system that prevented any but approved pictures or stories from reaching the home front.[31]

From the perspective of the Vietnam War (when the American press faced few restrictions and the military lost) and the Falkland Islands War (when the British completely managed the press and its military won), the American government and military believed there was a lesson to be learned. There had to be severe restrictions, or the media would lose the next war, too.

In 1983 American troops invaded the Caribbean island of Grenada, and the military, in the person of Commanding Admiral J. Metcalf III, excluded all reporters from the combat zone for two days, insisting that this was done only for the reporters' protection. When some enterprising correspondents rented a boat and tried to evade the restrictions, American planes flew mock bombing missions against them, and an American naval vessel detained them. Reporters were allowed onto the island only after the brief fighting was over, and escort officers allowed them to travel only to approved areas. The American public was fed a diet of officially approved information, including nothing but positive information. The fact that American planes had mistakenly bombed a hospital was suppressed, as was the fact that military planning had been faulty and opposition had been practically nonexistent.

President Ronald Reagan's secretary of defense, Casper Weinberger, justified it all by saying that the military opposed having reporters along during the invasion, and he "wouldn't ever dream of overriding a commander's decision." Despite the tradition of civilian control of the military and of the presence of reporters in every American war, the Reagan administration stood history on its ear and established the most thorough prior restraint possible, i.e., total exclusion. The American nation approved heartily, the public supporting the military's anti-press actions five to one in one poll and eight to one in another. An American admiral correctly surmised, "Actually all the public really cares about in the long term is that we won." A press secretary of the previous Carter administration put it more graphically. "It was sometimes difficult to tell," he said of Grenada, "which the American people enjoyed more, seeing the President kick the hell out of the Cubans or the press."[32]

Although the military and political leadership had achieved a complete anti-press triumph in Grenada, the press protested, a House subcommittee held a hearing, and even some military leaders believed that the restrictions had gone too far. In 1984 General John W. Vessey, Jr., the chairman of the Joint Chiefs of Staff, established a commission headed by retired army general Winant Sidle, a former press officer during the Vietnam War. Vessey told this Media-Military Relations Panel, usually called the Sidle Panel, to find an answer to the long debated question, "How do we conduct military operations in a manner that safeguards the lives of our military and protects the security of the operations while keeping the American public informed through the media?"

The panel's report was not what the military wanted to hear. It stated that the media had to be present in any future war, although in a way that insured operational security and troop safety. The military should use a media pool, the panel wrote, until a wider number of reporters could arrive on the scene. In all cases, the military should provide adequate logistical support. As for reporters, "The basic principle governing media access should be compliance with predetermined ground rules issued by the military." In short, the military should allow reporters in, said the Sidle Panel, but the correspondents must follow the rules the military established and accept the concept of a Department of Defense National Media Pool under military supervision.

The media seemed content, in its lack of unity, to depend on what it believed were inviolate constitutional guarantees. It refused to take any seats on the Sidle Panel because of concern that such service might force automatic acceptance of any decision the panel promulgated. When the United States launched air strikes against Libya in 1985, no pools were established, despite the Sidle Panel principles, so the press was once more shut out. Ominously, a Pentagon official responded to media protests by saying: "Sidle doesn't commit us to anything."[33]

Little changed when sixteen thousand U.S. troops, the largest American military operation since Vietnam, invaded Panama on December 20, 1989, in Operation Just Cause, the action organized to capture Panamanian strongman Manuel Noriega. In theory the National Media Pool was to be activated, but in practice, the administration of President George Bush and its military leaders kept the media away in ways that had proven so successful in Grenada. The recommendations of the Sidle Panel report were ignored. Logistical support for reporters was lacking, the temporary pool arrangement became permanent, reporters who did make it into the pool were delayed in reaching the conflict area, and then they were kept away from the fighting. There were reporters on the scene, permanently stationed in Panama, but they were not included in the pool and were excluded from the action even more completely than the pool reporters. The military kept reporters in a windowless room and subjected them to meaningless briefings and reports from the Cable News Network (CNN) on television. The Pentagon provided whatever film or photographs it wanted the nation to see; reporters and photographers could not take their own pictures or interview wounded Americans or captured Panamanians. As in Grenada and despite the Sidle Panel, the military kept the press far away from the conflict and prevented it from providing meaningful information to the American public. Despite the claims of Secretary of Defense Richard Cheney about the precise bombing of the Stealth aircraft, for example, the plane actually performed poorly. Deaths from friendly fire and from low altitude parachute jumps also remained secret. General Sidle said, with disbelief, "If you're going to let the media in you have to let them do something."[34]

Once again the press was furious. In response, Assistant Secretary of Defense for Public Affairs Pete Williams asked Fred Hoffman, a veteran Associated Press Pentagon reporter and between 1987 and 1989 a deputy assistant secretary of Defense for Public Affairs, to find out why the pool system had failed so miserably. Hoffman issued his report in December 1989 and placed major blame on Secretary of Defense Cheney for what he termed "excessive secrecy." He also listed seventeen recommendations to prevent another fiasco in the future, reiterating the main thrust of the Sidle Panel report, calling, once again, on political and military leaders to include press coverage in any future planning or execution of military action. Public Affairs officers, Hoffman said, should be included in battle planning from the start and should aggressively argue with the secretary of defense and the chairman of the joint chiefs of staff against secrecy and for a full media role. In March 1990 the joint chiefs of staff issued a new statement supporting the pool system and telling commanding officers to make sure that the public received maximum information in any future war. Details were left for later development, but the media once again did not zealously insist that their rights be insured.[35]

The result was that when the United States fought Operation Desert Storm, the brief Persian Gulf War, official administration and military policy continued to exclude reporters and manage the news, as had been the case in Grenada and Panama. There was, according to an editor of the *Washington Post*, "censorship by delay," "death by briefing," "blacking out the ugly parts," and "leakproof pools," all of which resulted in the American public knowing only what officials wanted it to know. The military enforced security review of reporters' copy, clearly a use of prior restraint, threatening denial of future pool privileges for any lack of cooperation. In one case, the military blindfolded a reporter for not staying with his pool. More usually, it simply kept reporters away from the action through the use of escorts, causing reporters to sit in their hotel rooms waiting for something to happen or talking to soldiers who were afraid to speak in front of an escort officer. During the Persian Gulf War, eighteen hundred television hours of war coverage, much of it on twenty-four-hour CNN, showed smart bombs, antiseptic warfare, and American troops apparently killing no one and suffering no casualties of their own. A critic wrote after the war that "the version of the Gulf War sent back to the United States by the press corps bore about as much resemblance to the real situation as a Disneyland exhibit does to the outside world, . . . a fantasy land image of the war that the Pentagon wanted the public to see."

According to one reporter, a senior Pentagon official told him that this was just the way it had to be. "If we let people see that kind of thing [killing and carnage], there would never again be any war."[36]

What became clear to reporters, as it had become clear in every previous war in American history, was that the individual commander in the field was the determining figure in the treatment of reporters. Even if superior officers supported complete media access, which was certainly not the case in the Persian Gulf War, an individual commander could keep reporters out if he wanted to. A Public Affairs officer, who wished to remain nameless, told a scholar in 1994: "There are no hard and fast rules (to allowing journalists into combat situations). What happens is up to the commander on site. Each situation is different and so are the rules."[37]

Immediately after the war's end, fifteen bureau chiefs in Washington criticized the treatment of the media in the Persian Gulf War, protesting to the Defense Department, "The virtual total control your Department exercised over the American press will become a model for the future." In September 1991, a subcommittee of this group issued a statement of principles and approached Secretary of Defense Cheney to negotiate an improvement of media-military relations. For the next eight months, negotiations went on, and in May 1992 the Pentagon issued new guidelines. On paper, this statement once again seemed to guarantee freedom of the press in time of war, except for the Pentagon's refusal to give up the practice of prior review of all press material before its release to the public. The media refused to accept this principle, but expressed pleasure at the statement as a whole. The military promised it would do better, but within four months it once again stepped back from some of its promises.[38]

What the media would do was another crucial question, however. Reporters covering the Persian Gulf War, like those involved in earlier skirmishes in Grenada and Panama, were hardly paragons of virtue or knowledge. A former Vietnam reporter, later an administrator at the Library of Congress, viewed the press performance in the Persian Gulf War with utter disdain. "They're ahistorical: they can't remember any precedents for anything." When they interviewed someone, he said, they practiced "'boo-hoo journalism' that is, asking How do you feel? Not What do you know? They're looking for that little emotional spurt. They don't know what the wider vignette means. They're yuppies in the desert." "Even after the shooting was over and reconstruction of the realities known," a scholar noted, "once again, the major news media failed to collect all the facts and present them in a coherent way that would effectively correct the misleading and inadequate information the public had been given earlier."[39]

Pentagon Public Affairs leader Pete Williams believed that what had occurred in the Persian Gulf War was "the best war coverage we've ever had." Newsman and former Vietnam War hero Colonel David H. Hackworth, on the contrary, said, "I think that truth and the freedom of the press took a tragic beating during the Gulf War," a view shared by esteemed newsman Walter Cronkite. The retired CBS television anchor told the public, "With an arrogance foreign to the democratic system, the U.S. Military in Saudi Arabia is trampling on the American people's right to know."[40]

So, what did the people think? According to polls taken during the Persian Gulf War, 80 percent of the American public were pleased with news coverage of the war, 79 percent thought that military censorship of the press was a good thing, and 57 percent thought the military should make its control over reporters even stiffer. Seventy-five percent did not believe that the military was suppressing bad news, being more worried that the press was giving the enemy valuable information. In short, the public overwhelmingly applauded the military's suppression of the media, and the military found this position supportive of its press policies. General Norman Schwarzkopf, the American commander in the Persian Gulf, said after the war that the American public had a right to know but that the media should ask that same public exactly how much it wanted to know.[41]

Little has changed in the years since the Persian Gulf War. Peter Arnett, who gained fame by remaining in Baghdad when American bombs were falling there, found himself attacked in front of the American Embassy in Haiti a few years later. American officials made no effort to help him, one of them later telling Arnett that his death would have given the American government just what it needed to intervene on the island. Yet, in the American intervention in Somalia and Haiti, reporters believed that their access and ability to publish information had improved vastly, though the old issues did not go away. The media coverage of the landing of marines, reporters using bright lights and noisy camera crews, proved shocking, as did the March 1993 press coverage of a Somalian mob dragging the body of a dead American helicopter pilot through the streets of Mogadishu. The scene of horrible death and mutilation hardly helped further the official desire to show war as antiseptic.[42]

Certainly that horrible scene helped mobilize the public outcry that led to the American withdrawal from the African country. In a future conflict, therefore, will the government and the military be willing to allow the media to send another such message to the American public? Will Somalia be to the future what Vietnam has been to the recent past, a lesson that the media must be totally controlled if a military effort is to be successful? Or will it perhaps be recognized, as one analyst of media military relations stated, that if an argument can be made that "an unfettered press may sometimes undermine a military operation," what about "the opposite possibility: that unwise policies that go unexamined or unchallenged may lead to needless death and suffering."[43]

And so, despite the passage of over a hundred years, the question of the press in war is very much what it was during the Civil War. The Supreme Court has not conclusively dealt with the issue of the First Amendment in wartime; Congress has passed no laws; and political and military leaders have successfully implemented restrictive practices during several wars. As in the past, therefore, this nation of laws still depends on the whims of man in the crucial area of First Amendment rights in war.

NOTES

1. *Schenck* v. *U.S.* 249 U.S. 47 (1919).
2. *Abrams* v. *U.S.* 250 U.S. 616 (1919).
3. *Pierce* v. *U.S.* 252 U.S. 239 (1920).
4. Discussed in Zachariah Chafee, Jr., *Free Speech in the United States* (Cambridge, 1941), pp. 298-305.
5. *Near* v. *Minnesota* 283 U.S. 697 (1931).
6. *Nebraska Press Association* v. *Stuart* 96 S. Ct. 2791 (1976).
7. Pentagon Papers case, 91 S. Ct. 2140 (1971).
8. Ibid.
9. *United States* v. *Progressive, Inc.* 467 F. Supp. 990 (Western District of Wisconsin, 1979); Susan Sullivan Lagon, "The First Amendment versus National Security: Judicial Interpretations of the Prior Restraint Doctrine," doctoral diss., Georgetown University, 1992, pp. 164-67; Henry Cohen, *Press Restrictions in the Persian Gulf War, First Amendment Implications* (Washington, D.C., 1991), p. 9.
10. Lagon, pp. 167-90; quote from Michael Linfield, *Freedom Under Fire: U.S. Civil Liberties in Times of War* (Boston, 1990), p. 160; Ted Galen Carpenter, *The Captive Press: Foreign Policy Crises and the First Amendment* (Washington, D.C., 1995), pp. 128-30.
11. *Nation Magazine* v. *U.S. Department of Defense* 762 F. Supp. 1558 (Southern District of New York, 1991).
12. *Flynt* v. *Weinberger* 588 F. Supp. (District of Washington, D.C., 1984).
13. *JB Pictures, Inc.* v. *Department of Defense* No. 91-397 (District of Washington, D.C., 1991).

14. Cohen, 13-16; Jeffrey A. Smith, "The Sword is Mightier Than the Pen: The Lack of Constitutional Authority for Military Restrictions on the Press," paper presented to annual convention of Association of Education in Journalism and Mass Communication, Kansas City, 1993, pp. 2, 2n; Morgan David Arant, "Constitutional Implications of United States Government Restrictions on the Press in the Persian Gulf War," doctoral diss., University of North Carolina at Chapel Hill, 1994, p. 404.

15. Bruce E. Fein, *Significant Decisions of the Supreme Court: 1975-1976 Term* (Washington, D.C., 1977), p. 72.

16. Harold M. Hyman, *A More Perfect Union: The Impact of the Civil War and Reconstruction on the Constitution* (New York, 1973), pp. 66-68, chapters 7 and 8.

17. James G. Randall, *Constitutional Problems Under Lincoln*, rev. ed. (Urbana, 1951), pp. 30-31; Kentucky jurist quote from Hyman, p. 143. Hyman, in his discussion of the Civil War generation's view of the Constitution in war, goes into much more detail than Randall, but he also concludes that there were three basic interpretations. One view held that the Jeffersonian negative on government action must still apply (Chief Justice Taney held this in the *Ex Parte Merryman* case [1861]). The second interpretation was to set aside the Constitution during war, and the third held that the Constitution was binding in war, but it sanctioned extraordinary war powers. Ibid., pp. 99-100.

18. Randall, *Constitutional Problems*, p. 508.

19. Adolph O. Goldsmith, "Reporting the Civil War," *Journalism Quarterly* 33 (Fall 1956): 478; Randall, *Constitutional Problems*, p. 481.

20. Dana F. Kellerman, "Censorship of the Northern Press during the Civil War," master's thesis, University of Illinois, 1960, p. 60; Craig Tenney, "Major General A. E.

Burnside and the First Amendment: A Case Study of Civil War Freedom of Expression," doctoral diss., Indiana University, 1977, pp. 25-26.

21. J. Cutler Andrews, *The North Reports the Civil War* (Pittsburgh, 1953), p. 95; Randall, *Constitutional Problems*, p. 482; Quintus C. Wilson, "Voluntary Press Censorship during the Civil War," *Journalism Quarterly* 19 (September 1942): 251-52.

22. United States *Statutes at Large*, 2:366: *War of the Rebellion . . . Official Records of the Union and Confederate Armies* (Washington, 1880-1901), Ser. III, 1:390.

23. Joe Skidmore, "The Copperhead Press and the Civil War," *Journalism Quarterly* 16 (December 1939): 350; Tenney, "Burnside," *passim;* James G. Randall, "The Newspaper Problem in its Bearing upon Military Secrecy during the Civil War," *American Historical Review* 23 (January 1918): 320-21.

24. Andrews, pp. 547, 633; Louis M. Starr, *Bohemian Brigade: Civil War Newsmen in Action* (New York, 1954), p. 278.

25. *New York Tribune*, 26 May 1862; Hyman, p. 198.

26. Charles H. Brown, "Press Censorship in the Spanish-American War," *Journalism Quarterly* 42 (Autumn 1965): 581-90; Cedric Larson, "Censorship of Army News during the World War, 1917-1918," ibid. 17 (December 1940): 313-20; Edwin Emery, *The Press and America*, 3rd ed. (New York, 1962), p. 761.

27. Frank Luther Mott, *American Journalism; A History 1690-1960*, 3rd ed. (New York, 1962), p. 761; Dale Minor, *The Information War* (New York, 1970), p. 6.

28. Leta Yvonne Deyerle, "A Public Relations Model for the Department of Defense during Combat Contingencies," master's thesis, Ohio State University, 1990, pp. 39-43; John R. MacArthur, *Second Front: Censorship*

and Propaganda in the Gulf War (Berkeley, 1993), p. xii; Carpenter, p. 155.

29. Shannon E. Crabtree, "Guidelines for Journalists in Future Military Conflicts," master's thesis, University of Houston, 1995, pp. 20-28; Deyerle, p. 57; Linfield, p. 141; Mark Hillel Samisch, "Comparison of the Media Coverage of the Vietnam War to the Media Coverage of the Invasions of Grenada and Panama: A Question of Legacies," master's thesis, University of Maryland at College Park, 1991, p. 9; Frank Aukofer and William P. Laurence, *America's Team, the Odd Couple: A Report on the Relationship Between the Media and the Military* (Nashville, 1995), p. viii.

30. MacArthur, 15; Carpenter, pp. 159-84.

31. Jacqueline E. Sharkey, *Under Fire: U.S. Military Restrictions on the Media from Grenada to the Persian Gulf* (Washington, D.C., 1991), p. 4.

32. Ibid., pp. 24-29; Smith, pp. 37-38; J. Metcalf III, "The Press and Grenada," in Peter R. Young, ed. *Defence and the Media in Time of Limited War* (Portland, Ore., 1992), p. 173; Crabtree, pp. 33-34. In Grenada, the 784 Cubans were construction workers building an air strip.

33. Pascale Combelles-Siegel, *The Troubled Path to the Pentagon's Rules on Media Access to the Battlefield: Grenada to Today* (Carlisle Barracks, Pa., 1996), pp. 4-7; Crabtree, pp. 12-14, 36-38; Sharkey, pp. 15-17; Timothy H. Hoyle, "Defending the News Media's Right of Access to the Battlefield," master's thesis, Michigan State University, 1996, p. 6.

34. Crabtree, pp. 39-41; Linfield, p. 159; David Wayne Lynch, "Twentieth Century Military-Media Relations: Censorship, Openness, Exclusion and Control," master's thesis, University of Tulsa, 1996, p. 71; Debra Lynn Pressley, "Us versus Them: A Survey of Army Public Affairs

Officers and the Press," master's thesis, University of Tennessee, Knoxville, 1991, pp. 34-35; Sharkey, p. 5. Deyerle, pp. 72-95, admits that there were snafus in the military handling of the press but criticizes the unprofessionality of the media and sees no organized military plan to exclude reporters. She concludes that both sides had grievances. Hoyle, pp. 6-8, is much more critical of the military and the Bush administration, citing Secretary of Defense Richard Cheney's refusal to allow on-site reporters into the pool, while delaying the establshment of the pool coming from the United States.

35. Combelles-Siegel, pp. 10-11. Brief explanations of the seventeen proposals appear in Crabtree, pp. 42-46 and Deyerle, pp. 97-102.

36. Hoyle, p. 1; Crabtree, pp. 47-52; Gary W. Sheftlick, "Airwaves of Intelligence: Content Analysis of 'Desert Storm' Network News," master's thesis, University of South Carolina, 1994.

37. Combelles-Siegel, pp. 15, 24, 33; Crabtree, p. 59.

38. Combelles-Siegel, pp. 18-21; Carpenter, p. 220.

39. Pressley, p. 37; Ben H. Bagdikian, foreword to MacArthur, p. xvi.

40. Hoyle, p. 1; David H. Hackworh, "The Gulf Crisis: The Media Point of View," in Young, p. 182; Robert E. Denton, ed. *The Media and the Persian Gulf War* (Westport, Conn., 1993), p. 11.

41. Sheftlick, p. 6; David Lamb, "Pentagon Hardball: Military Restrictions on Press Coverage of Operation Desert Storm," *Washington Journalism Review* 13 (April 1991): 33-36; Sharkey, p. 29.

42. Julio C. Zangroniz, "Peter Arnett Pays Tribute to Civil War Reporters," *Civil War News* (December 1996): 12; Crabtree, pp. 56-57; Hoyle, p. 12; Madison quote in Smith, p. 27.

43. Carpenter, p. 259.

2
The Antagonists

THE GENERAL, obviously absorbed in thought, was pacing up and down the railroad platform. It was the fall of 1861 and the command of Union forces in a section of the key border state of Kentucky lay upon his shoulders. An undeterminedly large Confederate enemy stood to his front and to his rear was a Northern presidential administration and people he believed were unaware of the danger they faced. He fretted and he paced, trying to find some hope in what he saw as basically a hopeless situation. Should the enemy attack him in his position on Muldraugh's Hill, forward of Louisville, he was sure his forces would be overrun.

The approach of a man carrying a sheaf of papers interrupted his thoughts. F. B. Plympton, a reporter and later editor of the *Cincinnati Commercial*, introduced himself to General William T. Sherman and presented letters of introduction, including one from the general's brother-in-law, Thomas Ewing,

Jr. Plympton wanted Sherman's permission to remain in the area.

The general, looking up, scanned the letters and remarked: "Letter from Tom, eh?" Pulling out his watch, he continued: "It is eleven o'clock; the next train for Louisville goes at half past one; take that train; be sure you take it; don't let me see you around here after it is gone." Plympton, stunned by the reply, answered: "But, General, the people are anxious and it's not my business to tell anything but the truth of what I shall see here." Sherman, unimpressed, retorted with greater vehemence: "We do not want the truth about things; that is what we don't want. Truth, eh? No sir. You take that train to Louisville; we do not want the enemy any better informed about what is going on here than he is. Make no mistake about the train." With that, Sherman whirled and resumed his pacing, leaving in his wake a speechless reporter.[1]

William Tecumseh Sherman was born on 8 February 1820, the sixth child of Ohio Supreme Court Judge and Mrs. Charles R. Sherman.[2] Charles Sherman was a descendant of Revolutionary War leader Roger Sherman, and he greatly admired the talented Indian leader Tecumseh. He named his new son after him. The baby's brothers and sisters quickly shortened Tecumseh to "Cump," and Cump he remained to family members for the rest of his life.

Cump's early life in Lancaster, Ohio, was happy

and without major problem. When he turned nine, however, his father died, and lack of funds forced his mother to parcel out the children among friends and relatives. Cump suffered the least dislocation; he moved but a short distance up the hill from his old home to the residence of later famous politician Thomas Ewing. He had spent all his early years playing with the Ewing children and running in and out of their house, so the move was as untraumatic as circumstances could have permitted. The Ewings made him one of their own and even had him baptized into their Catholicism. (The Christian name William was added to his Indian one because his baptism took place on St. William's Day.)

Though he was always treated as a full member of the Ewing family, sometime during his life Sherman developed an aversion to dependence, to being a ward of the Ewings, a feeling that increased during adulthood. In many ways, in fact, his life was a struggle to free himself of Ewing help, direction, and support. He determined to become a success on his own.

This is not to imply that his early life was unhappy. Cump had a pleasant and instructive childhood. As Thomas Ewing grew in political prominence, his home correspondingly became a center for political activity. Leading members of the Whig Party stopped off at the Ewing home, and because of them and his foster father Cump developed a deep devotion to the Constitution and Union. It was perhaps at this time too that he acquired his life-long dislike of politicians. He had a reverence for the Union, but he never thought much of its practitioners.

When he became sixteen, his foster father, now a Senator, sent him to West Point. He viewed this development with little enthusiasm and spent four years (1836-1840) chafing under the stern Military Academy demerit system. His lack of "spit and polish" reduced his class rank, but he still finished sixth out of a class of forty-one. He was commissioned in the artillery, and, freed from Academy discipline, looked forward to happier military experiences. To his dismay, the Ewings, who had earlier insisted on his entering West Point, now told him to resign his commission and go into business. He rejected their advice; he decided to make the Army his career.

His first military assignment took him to the wilds of Florida, but later duty found him in more civilized places in the South like Charleston's Fort Moultrie. During one of his assignments, he physically inspected the area of his later march to the sea. He also came to know and admire southerners, and in letters home he even praised the institution of slavery. These experiences had a deep impact on him and influenced his thinking when it came time to command troops in a civil war against people he had come to know and admire.

When the Mexican War began Sherman wanted a combat position. Instead, to his disappointment and later discomfort, the young lieutenant was placed on recruitment duty in Pittsburg, Pennsylvania, and Zanesville, Ohio. He became so frustrated that one day he deserted his post and rushed off to an embarkation center. Army authorities ordered him back immediately. By the time he finally received orders for California and the war, the fighting was over. The only action he experienced consisted of aiding Army efforts to preserve law and order among squabbling Forty-Niner gold prospectors. This was hardly battle activity and later, during the Civil War, he felt himself severely handicapped by this lack of Mexican War combat experience.

Despite this disappointment, Sherman decided to remain in the Army. In 1850 he made another important decision. At Blair House in the presence of President Zachary Taylor and his Cabinet, of which Thomas Ewing was Secretary of the Interior, Sherman married his childhood friend and foster-sister, Ellen Ewing. This marriage made him even more than ever a member of the Ewing family, and he had the unusual distinction of having the same man as father-in-law and foster-father. His sense of dependence on the Ewings and his determination to be independent from them only increased. His wife did not want to live anywhere but in Lancaster, and the Ewings joined her in appealing to him to resign the Army and become manager of the family salt works there. He repeatedly refused, and she regularly left him to return with their children for long visits to the house on the hill in Ohio. These trips strained Sherman's finances and his emotions, but they only increased his determination to succeed without family help. His Army pay never seemed to be sufficient to support his growing family, so he began thinking of a business career. In

1853 at the age of thirty-three, despite a recent promotion to captain, he accepted an offer from a St. Louis banker and agreed to run a branch bank in San Francisco. His wife and family were displeased, but he did it anyway.

Unfortunately, the bank failed during the Panic of 1857. Sherman was disappointed but undaunted, and he set up a new branch in New York City. Again the Panic intervened, caused his bankruptcy, and even toppled the parent institution in St. Louis. This second failure so shattered his self-confidence that he agreed to return to Ohio and work for the family interests. At the last moment his foster brothers, Thomas Jr. and Hugh Ewing, invited him to join in a Kansas law practice, and, though he was not a lawyer, he jumped at the chance. Anything was better than the family salt works.

Failure again dogged him. He made a bad investment, and after becoming a lawyer he found he did not like the legal profession. He did not practice it long and certainly acquired little knowledge of constitutional law. He decided to return to the Army while his family once more urged him to return to Ohio. He applied for an Army pay-mastership instead but learned there were no openings. When a new military academy in Louisiana began looking for a superintendent, he applied for the position, was hired, and became one of the founding fathers of what today is Louisiana State University.

In mid-October 1859 Sherman pondered and rejected an offer to begin a bank in London and left for Louisiana as originally planned. He found the work of education satisfactory and the people congenial.

He looked with confidence to the future and began making preparations for bringing Ellen and the children to join him. Then the secession controversy blew a dark cloud onto his horizon. He opposed secession because of his ideal of order and his veneration for the Union, learned as a child in the Ewing home. He warned state officials that if secession came he would have to resign on principle. Louisiana seceded in early January 1861 and, despite the dismay of school officials, Sherman reluctantly gave up his post. His hopes were again shattered; again circumstances out of his control had ruined his plans. Sadly he left Louisiana and the job and the people he had come to love. He returned North and accepted a position as president of a St. Louis street railway company. At first, his disgust at the way the Federal Government was responding to the emergency kept him out of the military, but when the actual fighting began, he reentered the Army. He eventually became one of the war's heroes, but only after much turmoil and personal anguish, much of it the result of his unsettled early years.

In 1861, then, Sherman was a disappointed and unhappy man; his first forty-one years of life had been filled with frustration. He had lost a father at the age of nine and had spent most of his days being tossed from job to job under the lash of a disapproving wife and foster family. He came to feel that the fates were against him. When he was considering the London position, he facetiously expressed these feelings: "I suppose I was the Jonah that blew up San Francisco and it only took two months residence in Wall Street to bust up New York—and I think my arrival in London would be the signal of the downfall of that mighty empire." Another time he put it more dejectedly: "I look upon myself as a dead cock in a pit, not worthy of further notice, and will take the chances as they come."[3]

This sense of failure and doom was a prime factor in Sherman's subsequent Civil War career, particularly during the early years. Whenever problems developed, his previous experience with failure caused him pessimistically to expect more of the same. But now desperation made this pessimism worse; if he failed again, his entire life would be one of continued dependence on his family. The need for success and the fear of failure jointly occupied his being.

His marriage added to this burden. He wanted to support his wife and six children in the manner she had been accustomed to at home. He became most despondent during those times when it appeared he would have to look to his foster-father as he had during childhood. His wife's close attachment to her father and Ewing's repeated offer of the salt mine manager's post only exacerbated matters. Sherman morbidly feared having to accept his foster-father's genuinely sincere offer; he had to make a success of his life or find himself returned to the position of ward, albeit as salt works manager. Failure caused not so much a bitter taste in his mouth as it did a salty one.

Though this basic insecurity affected Sherman during his early years in the Army, observers were little aware of it. His striking appearance made more of an impression on his contemporaries than did anything else. He stood six feet tall with long arms and legs, sandy red hair, almost always mussed, a reddish beard, and a face that came to be more and more a corduroy of wrinkles as the years went by. His eyes were described as "restless and searching orbs," "keen and piercing," "kindly as a rule but cold and hard as steel sometimes."[4]

His personality and mannerisms, which were readily observable, gave a clue to the turmoil going on inside him. He was a man of intense purposefulness heightened by an overabundance of nervous energy, "a 'bundle of nerves' all strung to the greatest tension." He seemed never to be still. Fingers were constantly stroking his hair or beard, buttoning or unbuttoning his coat, or tapping rhythmically on any nearby object. He would first be sitting then in an instant pacing up and down. He smoked heavily, and his ever present cigar was less an idle pleasure than it was a venting of emotion. He attacked each cigar with a vengeance. He had a veritable compulsion for talk exhibited in short brisk sentences punctuated by a variety of gestures. He would interrupt another speaker without second thought but would not allow himself to be similarly interrupted. In giving orders, he would grasp a subordinate by the shoulders and, when finished, push him toward the door talking all the way. He spoke so quickly that often his meaning was lost in the torrent of words pouring from his mouth.[5]

Like his body, Sherman's mind was seldom at rest; while campaigning he slept little and was a familiar figure pacing in front of his campfire deep in thought. In foul weather, during his later famous marches, he would sometimes use a vacant house for his headquarters. His men would then see him, pacing up and down, his shadow cut by the light of a candle, head down, chin pushed forward, hands stuck in his pockets. "When Uncle Billy can't march by day, he marches all night," they would jokingly tell each other.[6]

During battle, these "ecentricities disappeared."[7] He gritted his teeth, clamped down on his cigar, and gave brief crisp orders; his entire being seemed focused on his mission. Self-doubt and recriminations might come later, but during battle he was confident, aggressive, and all business.

Particularly during his marches, his soldiers came to look upon him with a great deal of good natured affection, "He's a queer old coon, but cant [sic] he just settle the Rebels," his clerk exclaimed. He had "no pomp nor [was he] stuck up, but common, everyday and right on the job all the while," another soldier wrote. Even some of his soldiers' songs expressed this confidence and admiration:

> Sherman, hurrah, we'll go with him
> Wherever it may be.
>   Through Carolina's cotton fields
> Or Georgia to the sea.[8]

Sherman never went out of his way to encourage such encomiums; in fact, his desire to stay out of the public limelight often created difficulties. He was so absorbed in his work that he had little time and even less desire to cultivate people. He was a diverse and talented man, in many ways an intellectual. "He was sometimes a dreamer, sometimes a practical businessman and organizer, and always an intensely combative commander."[9] He had many talents, yet he lacked self-confidence. His experience with failure and his intellectual's ability to see the many sides of problems caused him mental anguish throughout the war. He was frequently depressed when faced with difficulties, particularly when others could not see them with his clarity of vision. He worried that failure would continue to haunt him not only because of mistakes he might make but also because of circumstances and persons beyond his control. His depressions were expressions of disgust and frustration made more prominent by a strong streak of self-criticism. He demanded perfection in himself because he seemed to feel that only in this way could he prevent the failure he so dreaded.

Thus, when it came to war, Sherman felt it "must be fought effectively or not at all."[10] He loved the South but felt that any necessary means were justified in order to insure a quick Union victory and thus his own success. War to him was hell or, as he put it another time, "cruelty and you can not refine it."[11] The only way to stop the cruelty was to end the war as quickly as possible. The entire nation had to be organized; nothing should be allowed to obstruct the war effort. Anyone or anything which prevented the war's efficient conduct had to be eliminated. He considered the United States Sanitary Commission and the Christian Commission with their chaplains and nurses as unnecessary interferences in the war effort. State recruiting agents and special relief parties were other granules in his well-oiled military machine. But the greatest hindrances to efficient war-making were newspaper reporters. They did nothing for him nor for his men, they got in the way, and, worst of all, they provided the enemy with vital intelligence. They played no role in uniting the Northern populace behind the war; commanders' official reports and soldiers' letters home kept the North sufficiently informed to accomplish this. The man who is remembered in history as a pioneer of psychological warfare against an enemy populace and army did not appreciate the role of newspapers in maintaining public support on his own home front.

Sherman's early life provides a further clue to the intensity of his war long anti-press feelings. Newspapers had helped bring on or exacerbate several of his earlier failures. In San Francisco, when Sherman and his fellow bankers tried to restore public confidence in the face of an upcoming panic, they were temporarily stymied by a critical article which appeared in a local paper, the *Sunday Times*. The article was so inaccurate that the bankers considered it a blackmail attempt. Sherman, upon reading it, immediately climbed the stairs to editor James Casey's office on the third floor of his bank building. He bluntly told Casey he would throw him and his press out the window the next time such an article appeared. Casey took the hint, wrote no more articles on finance, and moved to safer quarters, presumably on the ground floor.[12]

Sometime later, Casey shot another newspaper editor as a result of a personal dispute. Perhaps hoping his political cronies would save him, Casey gave himself up. A vigilance committee was formed to prevent this from happening, and the city's press fanned the growing anger. Sherman had only recently accepted a major generalship in the state militia, but he was forced to stand helplessly by because this force was not strong enough to prevent the vigilantes from hanging Casey and an alleged accomplice. He blamed the city's newspapers for this anarchy and chaos, referring to the papers as "a perfect curse."[13]

During the Panic of 1857 Sherman temporarily closed his bank in what proved to be a futile effort to save it. A newspaper editor asked him to explain the closing, threatening to write a story with or without Sherman's help. Sherman prudently provided the information but felt the editor "expressed it somewhat awkwardly [sic], in three dailies, and I took it for granted deposits would be drawn instanter."[14] The bank was not affected by this article and did not fail until later. But Sherman was convinced once again of the press' ability to cause mischief.

Thus, in California, Sherman directly linked his failure to the activity of reporters. Newspapers had intervened to make a bad situation worse, to increase the strain he felt, and to help bring about his downfall. He learned to fear the press, to see newspapers as being capable of frustrating his deeply felt need for success. It was in California that the seeds of future press hatred were sown. Later, these seeds, watered by the sweat and blood of war, sprouted into full bloom. By then his experiences had convinced Sherman that newspapers were a genuine threat to the success of Union arms and therefore to his hopes of career fulfillment and success in life.

This attitude placed him in conflict with a burgeoning force in American life. Newspaper influence had been increasing since the inception of the "penny press" in the 1830s, and the Civil War continued, if not intensified, this development. Northerners depended on newspapers to keep abreast of the latest battle field developments, so the press' position in northern society grew more significant during the Civil War. At the same time, the newspaper itself was changing. Previously the editorial page had been the focus of greatest interest, but now the reporters' news columns became more important. As press influence increased in the nation, reporters' influence increased in the newspaper.[15]

This evolving situation intensified competitiveness among the journalistic fraternity. Newspapers and their reporters competed with one another to provide news more completely and more quickly, and the rivalry at times became cutthroat. Whoever won out would sell a large number of newspapers, make money, and be able to brag about it for several days afterwards. The pressure to succeed was a vital part of journalistic motivation.

The acknowledged leaders of the northern press were the New York City newspapers. Vying with one another in a bitter and often entertaining competition, the New York papers built up large organizations with numerous correspondents. The expense was enormous, but the profits proved to be great. Frederic Hudson, the managing editor of the *New*

York Herald, estimated that it cost his newspaper $525,000 to cover the Civil War, but the *Herald* also announced a rise of circulation from a prewar rate of 60,000 to 135,000 by 1863. The *Herald* had the largest number of reporters of any paper (at times numbering sixty-three in the field), but the *New York Times* and the *New York Tribune* were not far behind. Since it cost from $1,000 to $5,000 per year per correspondent, expenses quickly increased. Therefore, only the wealthier papers, like the ones in New York, could afford field correspondents and these had to produce to justify their cost. Smaller papers "clipped" (i.e., reprinted stories from the wealthier papers) or depended on the New York Associated Press or its rival the Western Associated Press. All papers, in a way they never had before, depended on the telegraph (the American Telegraph Company and Western Union) to rush them news stories for immediate publication.[16]

The *Herald* was the leading newspaper in New York City and thus in the nation too. It straddled most Civil War issues; it praised Lincoln one day, and supported McClellan, the general or presidential candidate, the next. It was the most popular newspaper in the Union Army because it provided the liveliest and most interesting coverage of the war. Led by its volcanic Scottish publisher, James Gordon Bennett, "The *Herald,* from its birth, was as peppery as a Mexican supper, and as intimate as a bathrobe."[17]

The *New York Tribune* was staunchly Republican. Still it often differed with Lincoln over his administration's slowness in emancipating the slaves and later his failure to develop a policy toward the freedman. It reflected its crusading head, Horace Greeley, and had an earnestness, dedication, and self-righteousness that was often irritating to those of opposing views. Its daily circulation of 55,000 and the weekly edition's 200,000 circulation were both spread over a large geographic area, so the *Tribune's* importance was national.[18]

The *New York Times*, under the leadership of sometime Republican Party chairman Henry J. Raymond, was consistently Republican. It was the one newspaper Lincoln could always depend on for support and, since its circulation of approximately 75,000 copies a day was significant, it proved to be a big help to the administration.[19]

The western center of the press was Cincinnati. Situated on the Ohio River at the northern terminus of the Louisville and Nashville Railroad, the "Queen City of the West" was in an excellent position to receive news from the armies fighting in that theatre. Its three leading newspapers were the Republican *Gazette* and *Commercial* and the Democrat *Enquirer*. Other newspapers further from the action often clipped these Cincinnati papers, and thus their influence transcended their region. The *Commercial* was particularly important because Murat Halstead, one of the great names in American journalism, was its publisher.[20]

These papers and others all over the North had one common characteristic. In order to obtain news from the front, they had to depend on the field correspondent. A man usually in his twenties, with better than average education, the Civil War reporter saw the war as an opportunity for rapid advancement in his trade or later in other professions. In the field he was a sight to remember:

> A man ... in mud-spattered mufti or Federal blue, astride the inevitable sway-backed nag—saddlebags bulging with mackintosh, notebooks, Faber No. 2's, field glasses, pipe, sometimes potables—riding amongst the troops with half an eye out for the provost marshal's men.[21]

The reporter's ragamuffin appearance often coincided with contemporary opinions of his worth. Ben Perley Poore, the famous Washington correspondent of the *Boston Journal*, thought: "There were honorable and talented exceptions, but the majority of those who called themselves war correspondents were mere scavengers." It often seemed that appreciation for the correspondent's trade and their daring was confined to the pages of the newspapers themselves. The *New York Herald*, for example, extolled its reporters in grandiose terms: "Homer was comparatively speaking a humbug. He never saw what he reported .... Homer and Milton did very well for old times, but the present age requires the *Herald*'s staff."[22] Actually, reporters were neither as good nor as bad as critics or supporters claimed. They were a tough-minded, able group under great pressure to produce, and they usually did.

Most reporters had good relations with the average Army officer and politician; they were usually welcomed around Army camps. Some officers even encouraged their presence because, as reporter Franc B. Wilkie cynically complained, "The majority of them were anxious to secure occasional notices of their whereabouts and their services."[23] Some officers ignored reporters, still others were powerless to affect them even if they felt hostility toward them. A number of generals and government officials were powerful enough to act against the press, and they imposed varying restrictions against reporters. In all, however, military and government attitudes varied widely.

Abraham Lincoln had favorable relations with reporters throughout the war, although he often received press criticism of the vilest kind. He was pragmatic enough to realize the press' power to hurt him and his administration, so he tried very hard to cultivate newspapers and their reporters. He put it this way:

> No man, whether he be private citizen or President of the United States, can successfully carry on a controversy with a great newspaper and escape destruction, unless he owns a newspaper equally great with a circulation in the same neighborhood.[24]

Edwin M. Stanton, Lincoln's Secretary of War, developed a hostile attitude toward reporters early in his term of office and was convinced that newspapers "no matter how useful or powerful," had to be "subordinate to the national safety." A specific encounter he had with a reporter clearly showed his hostility. A certain Dr. Malcolm Ives of the *New York Herald* appeared at the War Department one day demanding to see the latest war correspondence. When he was refused, he threatened press reprisals. Unimpressed, Stanton, who had previously caught Ives in the War offices spying, had him arrested. The *Herald*, rather than protesting, denied any association with Ives, and he was never heard from again. Stanton, however, was convinced that newspapers and their correspondents could not be trusted. As Lincoln related it to William Cullen Bryant, Stanton told him: "The New York papers must be reliable. For did they not keep lying and *re*lying?"[25]

Stanton's predecessor, Simon Cameron, had handled the press differently during his brief tenure of office. The *New York Tribune*'s Samuel Wilkeson praised Cameron profusely and, to make sure that Cameron knew it, sent him clippings with notes like: "The satisfaction of doing justice to a wronged statesman is not equalled by the pleasure with which I sincerely pay a tribute of respect to a maligned good man." Cameron responded by extending special privileges; Wilkeson was free from the telegraphic censorship other reporters labored under, and Cameron also often gave him exclusive information. Unfortunately for Wilkeson, when Stanton replaced Cameron, such ploys proved useless. He lost his privileges, becoming so exasperated that on one occasion he wrote his editor: "This senseless Censorship of the Telegram!! I can't get anything to you of interest.... Destroy the Censorship—destroy the Censorship."[26]

Ulysses S. Grant received mixed treatment in the press ranging from accusations of drunkenness and incompetence after the battle of Shiloh to the December 1863–March 1864 *New York Herald* presidential boom. Usually, he ignored reporters. He told them on one occasion: "You yourself must determine what is proper to send. I trust your discretion and your honor to give no information of value to the enemy."[27]

Most military men were not so generous. Henry W. Halleck, the later Union Chief of Staff, commanded in the West early in the war, and whenever he could excluded what he called "unauthorized hangers-on." He also appointed a specific officer to act as his command's official censor. General Ambrose Burnside not only closed down the *Chicago Times* for several days because of its editor's violent criticism of the Union war effort, but later he justified his actions by equating all such newspapermen with the armed enemy the Union army was battling. General Irvin McDowell told "Bull Run" Russell of the *London Times* that he would be happy to allow reporters into the field if they would wear white uniforms "to indicate the purity of their characters." General Benjamin Butler was not even humorous. He felt "the Government would not accomplish much until it had hanged . . . half a dozen spies, and at least one newspaper reporter."[28]

U. S. Navy officers lived in close proximity to reporters on board their ships, and thus they had greater control over them than did their Army counterparts. Still, they were so suspicious of the press that they made their official reports as nebulous as possible and sent more detailed information to the Secretary of the Navy confidentially. One naval officer even outdid his army colleagues in a statement of contempt toward the press. He described a *Herald* reporter as "a creature whose mere looks excite disgust and whose mind is in full sympathy with this degraded appearance."[29]

Sometimes the encounters between military men and reporters, though acrimonious, were also humorous. In September 1864 Phil Sheridan, the fiery hero of the Shenandoah Valley, stopped the *New York Times'* George R. Williams and protested the correspondent's report of a recent skirmish. He gave Williams twenty-four hours to get out of his department. The reporter responded that Sheridan's department included New York City. Sheridan exploded: "Oh, go to the devil if you like!" "Alright [sic] General," answered Williams, "but I am afraid I shall not be out of your district even with his Satanic majesty!"[30]

Throughout the war, then, reporters, government officials, and military leaders debated the press' role in the conflict. Individuals like Sherman were determined to keep intelligence from reaching the enemy, while newspapermen were equally determined to fight any infringement on their right to gather news. The problem was complicated by the lack of a widely accepted constitutional philosophy or historical experience with the issue; by the attitudes of individual military men in either enforcing, extending, or ignoring existing regulations; and by the varying quality, determination, and integrity of individual reporters. Correspondents who were smart enough to do so used this confusion to their advantage and were able to publish just about anything they wished. Some intelligence undoubtedly reached the enemy, but it was usually so mired in a plethora of detail it was difficult to decipher and thus of limited value to the Confederates.[31] Had there been no regulations at all, no threat of government suppression, however, the temptation to be first and to sell papers might have resulted in greater security problems than actually existed. But there is no proof that the total elimination of the First Amendment would have measurably shortened the war. Complete censorship might have rid the politicians and the generals of a great deal of frustration, but it would more probably have silenced much essential criticism.

When the Civil War began, then, even before the two antagonists had come into contact, it could have safely been predicted that William Tecumseh Sherman and newspaper reporters would find themselves in conflict. Because of the experiences of his pre-Civil War life, Sherman saw newspapermen as a threat to his last chance for success. Newspaper reporters viewed anti-press generals like Sherman as threats to their ability to perform their tasks and survive as efficient purveyors of battle news. When their interests came in conflict, the ensuing battle was inevitable. Both saw themselves as defending essential American principles— Sherman, the Union's survival; newspapers, the public's right to the news. Beneath the grandiose terms, never fully developed as a constitutional ideology by either antagonist, was a more basic fact. Both saw their contest with one another as a matter of personal survial.

NOTES

1. Murat Halstead, "Recollections and Letters of General Sherman," *Independent* 51 (15 June 1899): 1611-1612.
2. The factual material for this sketch of Sherman's life may be found in William T. Sherman, *Memoirs of General William T. Sherman* (New York, 1866), 1: 90–204. Hereafter cited as: Sherman, *Memoirs*. Sherman's two main biographers were also helpful: Lloyd Lewis, *Sherman: Fighting Prophet* (New York, 1932), pp. 1-161, and James M. Merrill, *William Tecumseh Sherman* (New York, 1971), pp. 15–161.
3. William T. Sherman to Ellen Sherman, 13 February 1860, Sherman Family Papers, University of Notre Dame Archives. Hereafter cited as: S. F. P., UNDA. WTS to ES, 15 April 1859, WTS, *Home Letters of General Sherman*, ed. M. A. DeWolfe Howe (New York, 1909), p. 159.
4. Thomas Wood, *Reminiscences of the War* (n.p., n.d.), p. 68; Noah Brooks, *Washington in Lincoln's Time* (New York, 1896), p. 318; James F. Rusling, *Men and the Things I Saw in the Civil War Days* (New York, 1899), p. 106.
5. W. F. G. Shanks, "Recollections of W. T. Sherman," *Harper's New Monthly* 30 (April 1865): 641–643, 646; Shanks, *Personal Recollections of Distinguished Generals* (New York, 1866), pp. 24, 54–55; Franc B. Wilkie, *Pen and Powder* (Boston, 1888), p. 160.
6. Henry Hitchcock, *Marching with Sherman*, ed. M. A. DeWolfe Howe (New Haven, 1927), pp. 112–113; Edward Corydon Foote, *With Sherman to the Sea: A Drummer's Story of the Civil War*, as related to Olive Dunne Hormel (New York, 1960), p. 183.
7. Jacob D. Cox, *Atlanta* (New York, 1882), p. 21.
8. Vett Noble, "Vett Noble of Ypsilanti: A Clerk for General Sherman," ed. Donald W. Disbrow, *Civil War*

History 14 (March 1968): 36; Elisha Stockwell, Jr., *Private Elisha Stockwell Jr. Sees the Civil War*, ed. Byron R. Abernathy (Norman, 1958), p. 98; S. H. M. Byers, *The March to the Sea: A Poem* (Boston, 1896), p. 21.

9. Allan Nevins, *War for the Union* (New York, 1971), 4: 26.

10. E. Merton Coulter, "Sherman and the South," *North Carolina Historical Review* 8 (January 1931): 54.

11. WTS to James M. Calhoun, Mayor, E. E. Rawson and S. C. Wells, rep. City Council of Atlanta, 12 September 1864, in WTS, *Memoirs*. 1: 126.

12. WTS to H. S. Turner, 2 July 1856, S. F. P., UNDA.

13. Ibid.; WTS, *Memoirs*, 1: 147–160; Doris Muscatine, *Old San Francisco* (New York: G. P. Putnam's, 1975), pp. 271–282; Hubert Howe Bancroft criticizes Sherman for his vigilante stand, and condemns him for "statements impeaching the integrity of California's purest and best citizens." Bancroft, *Popular Tribunals*, Vols. 36 and 37 of *The Works of Hubert Howe Bancroft* (San Francisco, 1887), 37: 284–289.

14. WTS to H. S. Turner, 19 April 1857, S. F. P., UNDA.

15. Marguerite H. Albert, "The New York Press and Andrew Johnson," *South Atlantic Quarterly* 36 (October 1927): 405; J. Cutler Andrews, *The North Reports the Civil War* (Pittsburg, 1953), p. 6; H. B. Babcock, "The Press and the Civil War," *Journalism Quarterly* 6 (March 1929): 1–3.

16. Dan Carlos Seitz, *Horace Greeley: Founder of the New York Tribune* (Indianapolis, 1926), p. 201; *New York Herald*, 14 February 1863; Frank Luther Mott, *American Journalism: A History 1690-1950* (New York, 1962), p. 332; W. F. G. Shanks, "How We Get Our News," *Harper's New Monthly* 34 (May 1867): 519; Dana F. Kellerman, "Censorship of the Northern Press during the Civil War," masters thesis, University of Illinois, 1960, p. 19.

17. Bernard A. Weisberger, *Reporters for the Union* (Boston, 1953), p. 18.

18. Ibid., p. 173; Frederic F. Endres, "The Northern Press and the Civil War: A Study in Editorial Opinion and Government, Military and Public Reactions," doctoral diss. University of Maryland, 1975, p. 49; Edwin Emery, *The Press and America*, 3rd ed. (Englewood Cliffs, N. J., 1972), p. 237n.

19. Andrews, p. 173; Endres, p. 59.

20. Andrews, pp. 27–28.

21. Ibid., pp. 61-63; Louis M. Starr, *Bohemian Brigade: Civil War Newsmen in Action* (New York, 1954), p. 57.

22. Ben Perley Poore, *Perley's Reminiscences of Sixty Years in the National Metropolis* (Philadelphia, 1886), 2: 127; *New York Herald*, 1 April 1863.

23. Wilkie, p. 263.

24. John Paul Jones, Jr., "Abraham Lincoln and the Newspaper Press During the Civil War," *Americana* 35 (July 1941): 469–470; see also Robert S. Harper, *Lincoln and the Press* (New York, 1951).

25. *American Annual Cyclopedia* (1863), 2: 509, quoted in Endres, p. 128; Emmet Crozier, *Yankee Reporters: 1861-1865* (New York, 1956), pp. 186–187; Harper, p. 132; Harry W. Peckham, *Gotham Yankee: A Biography of William Cullen Bryant* (New York, 1952), p. 152.

26. Samuel Wilkeson to Simon Cameron, 25 August 1861, quoted in Starr, p. 68; Cameron to H. E. Thayer (chief censor), 5 October 1861, quoted in ibid., p. 70; Wilkeson to Sydney Howard Gay, 19 December 1862, Sydney Howard Gay Papers, Butler Library, Columbia University.

27. David Q. Voigt, "'Too Pitchy to Touch': President Lincoln and Editor Bennett," *Abraham Lincoln Quarterly* (September 1950), p. 146; Starr, p. 276.

28. Thomas H. Guback, "Control and Censorship of the

Northern Press during the Civil War," bachelors thesis, Rutgers University, 1958, pp. 53–55; Kellerman, pp. 65–68; Craig Tenney, "Major General A. E. Burnside and the First Amendment: A Case Study of Civil War Freedom of Expression," doctoral diss., Indiana University, 1977; Crozier, p. 92; Weisberger, p. 79.

29. Richard West, "The Navy and the Press during the Civil War," *United States Naval Institute Proceedings* 63 (January 1937): 27–35; Louis M. Starr, "James Gordon Bennett: Beneficent Rascal," *American Heritage* 6 (February 1955): 36–37.

30. Andrews, pp. 600–601.

31. In James G. Randall, "The Newspaper Problem in its Bearing Upon Military Secrecy during the Civil War," *American Historical Review* 23 (January 1918): p. 303, this leading authority on Civil War press relations writes that the press "undoubtedly did the national cause serious injury by continually revealing military information, undermining confidence in the management of public affairs and giving undue publicity to the virtues of ambitious generals and the sensational features of the war." Despite this strong statement, Randall does not prove that press activities actually "cause[d] serious injury" to the Union's war effort. Andrews cites Randall in concluding that newspapers' "premature announcements of troop movements caused unnecessary battles and the needless expenditure of human lives" (pp. 648–649). Bernard Weisberger concludes that: "Some of the reporters for the Union seemed to be steering journalism toward the wastelands of ballyhoo, but others were pointing the way towards crusading newspaperdom" (p. 286). Weisberger's temperate view seems more accurate than Randall's and Andrews's harsh criticism.

3
"The Insane General"

WILLIAM T. SHERMAN sat in his St. Louis office early in 1861 a disappointed frustrated man. He was president of a street railway company, but the only satisfaction this job gave him was the ability to provide for his family without dependence on the Ewings. He was not as happy here as he had been as school superintendent in Louisiana. He had felt duty bound to resign that post when secession had come, and he hoped his sacrifice was worthwhile. When he had talked to President Lincoln on his way through Washington in mid-March, he had been shocked at what he considered was Lincoln's nonchalant attitude toward the whole crisis. His Senator brother, John, had arranged the interview, and Sherman told him later that Lincoln was not taking southerners seriously enough; he was underestimating the difficulty of restoring the Union. Consequently, Sherman resolutely decided not to enter the Army or take any post with the administration. He could not bring himself to associate with another situation that might become a failure. He was determined to "bide" his time until "Professional Knowledge . . . [was] appreciated."[1]

Still, his sense of duty, shown in his decision to leave Louisiana, did not permit him the luxury of withdrawal. He offered the War Department his services but carefully attached several revealing conditions. He wanted to serve for three years in a Regular Army position, refusing any post with a volunteer unit because his anonymity would prevent his election as an officer. He also did not want a high post, believing his lack of Mexican War combat experience disqualified him for such responsibility.[2] Sherman wanted a secure position without great responsibility and with the least risk. (Certainly his refusal to join a volunteer unit indicated his desire to avoid those least prepared for war and thus most prone to failure.) His conscience and his sense of duty urged him to aid his country, but his ego and his concern for his future limited the role.

At the urging of his family he went to Washington in May to check on his application, and he found that his assignment fit his conditions. He was appointed a Colonel, Thirteenth Regular Infantry, Washington. Lack of experienced officers quickly forced a change, however, and authorities made him a brigade commander. His fears had been realized: he had a high combat responsibility for which he felt he was unqualified, in a war led by civilians whose judgment he did not trust, against an enemy he considered as "kind good friends."[3]

He could have resigned, but this would have once again indicated failure. He had no choice; he had to take on the responsibility. When he faced his first stress situation, he reacted well. He overcame his fears to play a leading role in stemming the Union panic at the Battle of Bull Run in July 1861. Still, the engagement in the Virginia countryside intensified his anxieties. At Bull Run, he saw what he had previously only feared; lack of Union preparation and poor leadership. The Union cause, for which he had sacrificed his Louisiana hopes and on which he had staked his future, was in even graver danger than he had supposed. "The Southern people are in earnest whereas our people mostly are in search of a political promise in the future," he complained. His anxiety became so evident that even George McClellan, the new Union commander, noticed it. While inspecting his troops upon assuming command, McClellan found Sherman "somewhat nervous" and intent on convincing him of the enemy's nearness. McClellan rode some distance past the Union pickets, "found no enemy," and viewed his red-headed subordinate with a jaundiced eye.[4] He would remember this incident in the future.

Sherman, frustrated, anxious, fearful of the future, now took an action he was to repeat often during the course of the war. He lashed out at newspaper reports of the battle. He had not even seen a newspaper, but he fumed that no reporter had the "Moral Courage to tell the truth," and newspapers would print "Ten thousand things none of which ... [were] true." They would blame Army officers for the Bull Run debacle instead of assigning fault where it belonged, on the shoulders of political leaders who were responsible for the disastrous unpreparedness. Even worse, he fretted, newspapers were daily printing secret information, and, as a result, Washington and St. Louis were in danger of enemy occupation.[5]

Here was a significant occurrence. Sherman attacked newspapers and their correspondents for reports he predicted they would write without first checking to see if they had actually written them. Obviously he was reacting to past experiences rather than to present facts. Earlier in his life, newspapers had intervened to worsen bad situations; therefore, they must have done it again. Sherman's first wartime experience intensified anti-press feelings he had developed before the war.

Feeling so upset over matters in the Washington area, Sherman was in a perfect frame of mind for a transfer. Such an opportunity soon presented itself. Robert Anderson, the hero of Fort Sumter, had recently been appointed commander of the newly created Department of the Cumberland and was searching for a top subordinate to aid him in his organizational tasks. Because of his family's connections with the president, Sherman was offered the position of brigadier general of volunteers. At a mid-August meeting with Lincoln, he accepted, but as he had done when he had first entered the Union army, he refused any present or future independent command. Considering his experiences with other Army officers, Lincoln was pleasantly surprised at this request. He quipped that there were not enough places to satisfy all the would-be leaders, so Sherman's condition was most welcome.[6]

The new brigadier general of volunteers left the meeting, gathered together his belongings, and left for Kentucky and his new post, happy to be leaving the confusion of Washington. He carried a heavier load than the usual soldier's baggage: self-doubt exhibited in his desire to hold no independent command, lack of confidence in Union leadership, love for the South, and a recognition of southern determination to survive outside the Union. Ever present, besides, was his obsession to reverse his lifetime of failure and become a success without Ewing help. His dislike for the press had also been intensified. The forty-one-year-old brigadier entered Kentucky with a great deal of anxiety placed upon his normally excitable personality.

Kentucky was one of the worst places for a man of Sherman's disposition. Affairs in the Bluegrass state were even more confused and disorganized than they were in Washington. The state and her people were badly split over the issue of the war. The Governor sympathized with the Confederacy, while the legislature was pro-Union. Enemy troops would sometimes take the same trains or be seen marching in opposite directions down the same street. Kentuckians revered the Union, but they also had ancient ties to the South. The solution to this dilemma was to declare neutrality. *Louisville Journal* poet-editor, George D. Prentice, described his fellow citizens as "supine and inactive." "They appear to be dead in spirit. They seem as if they would gladly lie down upon their beds and sleep away all the bloody days and weeks and months and perhaps years that are before us. They shrink and cower and stand appalled at the presence of the fearful crisis." Both Federals and Confederates in Kentucky were unhappy with the size of their forces, each "grossly overestimated the strength of the other, and each worked frantically to prepare for an attack by its supposedly more numerous foe." There was much Confederate sympathy within Kentucky, but the Confederacy's violation of the state's neutrality helped cause more Kentuckians to enlist in the Union Army than in the Confederate: 90,000 for the Federals to somewhere between 25,000 and 40,000 for the Confederates. The 5 August 1861 legislative elections resulted in a seventy-six to twenty-four edge in the House and a twenty-seven to eleven edge in the Senate for the Unionists. Still, by the end of 1861, only about 29,000 spots in the proposed 42,000-man Union force had been filled, and military supplies were in short supply. On the Confederate side, the problems were even greater and, though it was not obvious to those present, the Union's inadequate numbers and supplies were still superior to those of the Confederates.[7]

On his arrival in late August, Sherman did not have the advantage of historical hindsight nor even adequate intelligence. His own eyes saw a weak Union position; therefore, it seemed reasonable to him that the Confederates had to be stronger. Confederate General Albert Sidney Johnston's seemingly aggressive movements masked his actual weakness and fooled Sherman even more as to his true strength.[8]

Sherman's difficulties in trying to raise men and supplies only intensified these feelings. Anderson sent him on a tour of the Indiana and Illinois state capitals and John C. Fremont's headquarters in Missouri, but he was unsuccessful. He noted much war activity everywhere he went, but when he tried to siphon off some of the men and material for Kentucky, he was politely rebuffed. He returned to Louisville empty-handed and bitter at "Northern Politicians [who were] constantly praising the resources and population of the North" but who were doing nothing to provide them to the Army.[9]

Although discouraged, he dove into the task of securing and organizing available men and supplies. He slept little, did not eat properly, and even went long periods without having time to change into clean clothes. What worried him most were rumors that Confederate General Simon Buckner, part of Johnston's command, was advancing into Kentucky from Tennessee.[10] Union forces were unprepared, and the Confederates were advancing; to Sherman, disaster seemed imminent.

In order to prevent a successful Confederate attack on Louisville, Anderson sent Sherman with a force of 7,000 men to fortify Muldraugh's Hill just outside the city. When he arrived there, his force dwindled to 5,000; the Louisville home guards deserted. The area's populace seemed openly pro-Confederate, and he had not resolved his own uncertainty about Buckner's size and plans. He continued to worry, and again he lessened his frustration by attacking the press. He tried to keep reporters away because he feared they would report his force's weakness and thereby invite a Confederate attack. It was at this time that he had his encounter with the *Cincinnati Commercial* reporter on the railroad platform. He also began to talk about needing a 100,000-man force to defend Kentucky properly.[11]

Newspaper correspondents were still new at war reporting, but they had already experienced government censorship and military hostility. Consequently it is doubtful whether they were shocked at Sherman's open animosity toward them. The *New York Times* even called Sherman "one of the most dashing officers of the Union."[12] When rumors spread that Anderson's poor health would cause his resignation and Sherman's promotion, reporters expressed confidence in his ability to do the job. His anti-press activities were not even mentioned.

The rumors soon proved correct. Robert Anderson's health had been impaired by his Fort Sumter experience and the pressure of Kentucky responsibilities, and he had to step down on 8 October. Sherman became commander of the Department of the Cumberland though he felt that it was "in direct violation of Mr. Lincoln's promise to me" and though he wished he could hide himself "in some obscure place." The War Department assured him that Don Carlos Buell would replace him as soon as possible, but he did not take this promise seriously. He saw himself stuck in a command he did not want with too few and badly supplied troops. The horror of helplessly watching some of his men become sick and die from exposure and lack of proper food only added to his revulsion at his new responsibility.[13]

Newspapers seemed genuinely pleased with the change. There was little mention of the new commander's hostility toward reporters, and, instead, most papers agreed with the *Cincinnati Enquirer* that he was the "right man for the right place."[14] They were confident he would do a good job in his new post.

Despite his reluctance, Sherman assumed his new responsibilities. He felt depressed (or as he later termed it "unnecessarily unhappy"). He suffered from headaches which he blamed on too many cigars, too much sitting and writing, and not enough exercise. He was convinced that any enemy attack would annihilate his forces and make him once again a failure. He grew even more anxious to improve his situation since he was now ultimately responsible for it. He tried to rectify the deficiencies by writing to several Washington political officials, notably the president. He curtly told Lincoln of his "entirely inadequate" forces and supplies and ended with the single word "Answer." When he received no response, he became gloomier.[15]

Because he felt increased frustration at his inability to improve his military situation, Sherman seized the only avenue he saw open to him. In order to "conceal the weakness" of his forces, he intensified his anti-press campaign. He might not be able to strengthen his army, but he could keep the enemy from knowing about his weaknesses. Excluding reporters from his army simply meant the frustration of one class of spies. He wanted to neutralize all informers, but since he could not, he tried to plug at least the journalistic leak.[16]

His frustration and his obsession with his military deficiencies showed itself in his actions, and word of it began to spread. It was repeated how Sherman, after using a sergeant's cigar to light his own, absent-mindedly threw it away as though it were a match. Another time he showed up for a formation in a uniform topped by a stovepipe hat. Most of all, his nocturnal activity provoked whispers. Sherman was never much of a sleeper, and he seemed to sleep even less because of the stress of command. Every night he would arrive at the Louisville telegraph office of the New York Associated Press about nine o'clock and wait for the latest dispatches until the early morning hours. He would freely complain to anyone present, often inconsistently to a reporter, the later railroad builder, Henry Villard. He would first be sitting, then pacing, constantly puffing on his cigar, seeing every danger, as Villard remembered it, with an "imagination inherent to genius." At 3 A.M. when the office closed, he would return to his lodging at the Galt House where he continued his pacing in the corridor leading to his room. Rumors began to spread that he was suffering some sort of a mental problem.[17]

Surprisingly, newspaper reporters' reaction to Sherman's activities, even his anti-press ones, were minimal. One reporter wrote a mildly critical article but ended it by praising Sherman for "achieving wonders" in Kentucky. *New York Times* reporter "Pontiac" compared Sherman to Napoleon, while the *Louisville Journal* editor praised him "to the skies" in letters to Ellen Sherman.[18] Sherman's anti-press animosity did not sufficiently hinder reporters, and therefore they were not angry enough to attack him in print. All seemed calm on the newspaper front; on the horizon, however, a storm was brewing.

Simon Cameron, the inept Secretary of War, was in Missouri trying to straighten out the mess John C. Fremont had caused there. As an afterthought, perhaps because of Sherman's earlier letters to Washington, he decided to stop in Louisville on his way back to the nation's capital. He was so tired from his trip that while talking to Sherman on 16 October 1861 he remained on his hotel bed throughout their conversation. Sherman saw a large number of strange faces standing around the room, and he hesitated to speak. Cameron urged him to be completely outspoken, promising that everyone in the room could be trusted. He neglected to mention that one of the loungers was his pet reporter, Samuel Wilkeson of the *New York Tribune*. Sherman locked the door and then bluntly complained of his shortages. The Secretary of War was upset at the news and ordered Adjutant General Thomas to send immediate help. When Sherman said he needed 200,000 men in order to go on the offensive, Cameron jumped up and asked where they were to come from. Sherman responded that plenty of men wanted to serve, but the administration was discouraging them. Cameron told Thomas to make a note of the conversation and promised Sherman further help. When the two men parted, the matter rested there.[19]

Two weeks later, on 30 October, the *New York Tribune* summarized this meeting in a report of Cameron's trip by Adjutant General Thomas. Rumor had it that Samuel Wilkeson was the real author of the statement, and its appearance in his newspaper was clearly no coincidence. In the section dealing with Sherman, the report viewed the Kentucky general's call for 200,000 men as the cry of a panicky worrier. Cameron, on the other hand, was portrayed as wisely and calmly promising help and urging immediate offensive action against the Confederates in the Blue Grass State.[20]

Initial press reaction to this article was aimed against the *Tribune* more than against Sherman. The *Cincinnati Commercial*, for example, called the publication of such sensitive information "covert treason or insane folly." The reason for the restraint was the newsmen's general acceptance of the validity of Sherman's figure. A week after Cameron's visit, an unnamed *New York Tribune* reporter told of rumors that 250,000 troops would be stationed in Kentucky within the month. Other military men and politicians made similar projections.[21] Therefore, it made little sense to attack Sherman for repeating what others were saying. The true situation was unknown both to Sherman and to the press.

Yet in some ways, this Thomas report was the turning point in newspaper treatment of the general. Criticism now began to appear where previously there had been mostly praise. The *Chicago Tribune*, for example, ridiculed him on two separate days: "Sherman was wild in his estimate." The reason for this change was not exaggerated troop calculations as much as it was Sherman's personality. Newsmen began assailing his "sternness, abruptness and roughness" which, according to "Pontiac," was alienating some Kentuckians. A *Cincinnati Gazette* reporter compared Sherman's disposition to that of a Pawnee Indian, and the rival *Commercial* demanded an apology to the Pawnees. Significantly, however, the same article labelled Sherman "the superior of any military man in the west."[22] Newspapers were more critical than before, but they were hardly damning and their criticism was because of Sherman's personality not the Thomas Report.

Sherman felt mortified at the publication of the Adjutant General's statement, and he worried even more about his military position in Kentucky. He received a few more troops as a result of Cameron's visit, but the situation remained relatively unchanged. He again decided to complain to Washington. His letters and telegrams grew more pointed and even desperate. On three consecutive days he sent telegrams to McClellan demanding help, suggesting retreat across the Ohio River to prevent being cut off, and castigating both Kentuckians and Washington alike for their indifference. He told McClellan he wanted to return to his old brigade in Washington and confessed to his wife that "the idea of going down in history with a fame such as threatens me nearly makes me crazy, indeed I may be so now."[23]

McClellan, despite his own over-cautious inactivity, believed Sherman should not only hold Kentucky, but he should also advance into Tennessee. He became concerned over Sherman's telegraphic innundation and ordered daily reports. When these letters grew more and more desperate, and recalling Sherman's earlier fears in Washington, he sent his close adviser, Colonel Thomas M. Key, to determine the problem. Key reported that Sherman's mind was too unsteady for command. Official Washington soon translated this statement to mean that Sherman was insane. Assistant Secretary of War Thomas Scott put it bluntly. "Sherman's gone in the head, he's luny." Quickly, Don Carlos Buell replaced Sherman in Kentucky. The 13 November 1861 order did not call for Sherman's release from the Army nor medical help but simply directed him to report to General Henry W. Halleck in St. Louis.[24] The allegedly insane general was being sent to another critical area of the war.

The transfer caught newspapers completely by surprise. Reporters had witnessed Sherman's eccentricities and some may have jokingly wondered about them, but apparently they did not take them seriously. When Sherman was relieved, newspapers groped for the reason, the *New York Times* even doubting whether any replacement would be his equal. The *Cincinnati Commercial*'s reaction, however, was prophetic. At first it blamed his departure on "the indiscreet and disgraceful publication" of his conversation with Cameron, but two days later on 11 November it criticised his "absolutely repulsive" manner and his lack of greatness. On 16 November a *Commercial* correspondent held nothing back. In an unsigned article, he called Sherman "a perfect monomaniac on the subject of journalism" with a "narrow mind" incapable of handling matters in Kentucky. Now that Sherman was leaving Kentucky, this unnamed newsman felt patriotism no longer prevented him from criticising the general's anti-press prejudice.[25]

This statement was the strongest criticism yet launched against the general, and it included a thinly veiled assault on his mental state. Significantly, however, no other reporter joined in: the *Commercial* article was an isolated statement. Reporters once more restrained themselves from an all-out attack on a nemesis. But the criticism had grown more severe, and this fact indicated the increasing loss of reporters' patience.

In the meantime, Sherman had sunk deeper into depression. He contemplated suicide, staying his hand only because of love for his children. The last few days before his move to St. Louis, his state of mind so frightened his staff that they wrote to his father-in-law for help. Ellen and two of the children rushed to his side, and so did John Sherman. They took him to a doctor, but no record of his evaluation and advice was preserved. The family left, and Sherman moved to his new assignment, increasingly ashamed of his Kentucky performance.[26]

Upon arriving in Missouri around 23 November, Sherman was sent to inspect troops in the Department and found them too scattered to his liking. He recommended a consolidation. Halleck said no and ordered him back to headquarters. When he arrived, he was humiliated to find his wife waiting for him. Ellen Sherman had come to St. Louis because he had not been answering her letters. She now insisted that he take a leave and come home. Faced with her insistence and the military scepticism toward his consolidation recommendations, he gave in. He took a twenty-day leave on 2 December and returned to Lancaster, Ohio, again a failure, again forced to depend on the Ewings. In military circles, he left behind the impression he had panicked in Missouri as he had in Kentucky. Halleck told McClellan: "it would be dangerous to give him a command" at this time because his "physical and mental system" was "completely broken by labors and cares." Halleck also said that Sherman had been stampeding the troops; but, soon after, he made precisely the troop movements Sherman had recommended.[27]

Home in Lancaster, away from the pressures of war, Sherman began to put matters into perspective. His disposition improved until he saw a *New York Times* column citing "disorders" for his removal "perhaps permanently" from his post. He grew more upset again. The depression returned in full force on 11 December when the *Cincinnati Commercial* announced his failure to the world in the bluntest way; he had failed, the paper said, because his mind had given out. The headline screamed:

GENERAL WILLIAM T. SHERMAN INSANE

> The painful intelligence reaches us in such form that we are not at liberty to discredit it that General W. T. Sherman, late commander of the Department of the Cumberland, is insane. It appears that he was at times, when commanding in Kentucky, stark mad. We learned that at one time he telegraphed to the War Department three times in one day for permission to evacuate Kentucky, and retreat into Indiana. He also on several

occasions frightened the leading Union men of Louisville almost out of their wits by the most astounding representations of the overwhelming forces of Buckner, and the assertion that Louisville could not be defended. The retreat from the Cumberland Gap was one of his mad freaks. When relieved of the command in Kentucky he was sent to Missouri and placed at the head of a brigade at Sedalia, where the shocking fact that he was a madman was developed, by orders that his subordinates knew to be preposterous, and refused to obey. He has, of course, been relieved altogether of command. The harsh criticisms which have been lavished upon this gentleman, provoked by his strange conduct, will now give way to feelings of deepest sympathy for him in his great calamity. It seems providential that the country has not to mourn the loss of an army through the loss of the mind of a general into whose hands was committed the vast responsibility of the command in Kentucky.[28]

This time other newspapers did not shy away. Unlike previous occasions, they attacked Sherman fully and in some cases savagely. The *Commercial* "insanity" charge was published in papers all over the country. Reporters also took the opportunity to vent their animosity in their own articles. A *New York Herald* reporter in St. Louis wrote that Sherman had "been known for many years as an extreme [sic] eccentric man and liable to all sorts of freaks of judgement." The *Cincinnati Gazette*'s soon to be famous reporter Whitelaw Reid ("Agate") said that he had always considered Sherman "a self-absorbed military enthusiast or a monomaniac." There was something very strange about him," Agate said, "and ... his eye had certainly a remarkable expression." However, stories that Sherman had been "stark mad" in Kentucky were "exaggerations." "His insanity was not clearly developed until his arrival at Sedalia [Missouri]." *Frank Leslie's Illustrated Newspaper* was the most succinct of all. It wrote: "General Sherman, who lately commanded in Kentucky, is said to be insane. It is charitable to think so."[29]

At the time, editors and reporters said they printed the insanity charge out of patriotic duty. They were serving their country by alerting the public and Union officials that an insane general was in command of a delicate area of operations. Their only desire was to insure Kentucky's safety against any disaster that Sherman's mental imbalance might have caused. They said nothing about punishing a strongly anti-press military man at a time when it seemed safe to do so. Later journalistic reminiscences indicated little altruism and a good deal of sloppy reporting. A number of reporters mistakingly remembered (and some later historians have repeated the mistake) that the insanity charge was published immediately after the Cameron visit in retaliation for Sherman's threat to hang a reporter. Another later view held that Cameron told Wilkeson that he believed Sherman was crazy and this reporter initiated the charge. Sherman himself blamed the attack on the revenge of a reporter he had imprisoned in Louisville.[30]

Murat Halstead, the editor of the newspaper which first made the accusation, said his *Cincinnati Commercial* printed the story because Henry Villard had told him that Kentuckians wanted someone to "bell the cat" before it was too late. In his reminscences, Villard disagreed. He said he had indeed told Halstead about the insanity rumors but had written to him as Sherman's friend not as *Commercial* editor. "But Halstead could not resist the temptation of utilizing the sensational information for his paper," Villard said, and that was why he had written the editorial.[31] Clearly then, the insanity charge was based on unsubstantiated hearsay. Newspapers printed it because its sensational nature might sell papers and also eliminate an openly anti-press general.

Still, the questions remain: did Sherman suffer from insanity, did he lose control of his mental processes, and was the press correct in pointing this fact out to the public? Sherman was obviously anxious and depressed, but these facts do not justify the charge that he was insane.[32] He never lost control of himself; he suffered no derangement. The facts used to prove his insanity were either exaggerations or inaccuracies. He never telegraphed Washington three times in one day, nor did he hold a command position in Missouri nor retreat from the Cumberland Gap. Though Halleck at first rejected Sherman's recommendations for consolidating troops, he later followed them.

As has been shown, Sherman was normally an intense man driven by a complexity of forces. At this time, he did suffer an extended neurotic anxiety reaction complicated by depression. The depression was exogenous rather than endogenous, that is, it was caused by real not imaginary problems. It was a very severe depression as evidenced by Sherman's contemplation of suicide, but it was not psychotic. Had Sherman developed a psychosis, concern for his children, for example, would not have prevented him from taking his own life.

A neurotic depression of an exogenous nature, such as Sherman apparently experienced, is often the result of suppressed anger over some frustration. Sherman's gloom was just that: frustration that conditions out of his control were again dooming his efforts and apparently again making him a failure. His depression was severe enough to make him consider suicide, but it was not deep enough to overwhelm his powers of concentration. On the contrary, it made him, already an intense person, become compulsive. He tried to compensate for his feelings of uncertainty and gloom by keeping active day and night; he slept little, paced, smoked, wrote letters to his superiors and complained to anyone who would listen. The lack of sleep and the heavy smoking only made matters worse. Sleep deprivation lowers body resistance and can lead to more anxiety, more depression, and poorer judgement. Sherman drove his tormented body and spirit to the point of exhaustion. He suffered no collapse, however; he was able to keep going despite his psychic problems.

It should also be remembered that in situations of extreme stress such as wartime, normal persons can and often do react with anxiety and depression as Sherman did. In war, too, persons often become more anxious during battle lulls (anticipatory anxiety) than they do in actual battle. This was the case with Sherman. During the battle of Bull Run, he performed well despite the presence of anxiety and depression both before and after the fighting.

During this period of his life, Sherman suffered from the simultaneous accumulation of a multitude of stresses and worries. When he had entered the Union Army, he had done so with little confidence in its leaders yet with an overwhelming desire to reverse his lifetime of failure. He had to succeed or return to his childhood dependence on Thomas Ewing. Throughout his married life, his wife's dependence on her father and her constant insistence that they live near him only exacerbated the problem. His immediate experiences in the Army intensified his fears of failure and made him concerned that, as in Louisiana, forces out of his control would once more destroy his hopes. His love for the South and his concern for his own soldiers must also be considered, the latter in light of his inferiority feelings over his lack of combat experience in the Mexican War.

In Kentucky, Sherman tried to insure success for Union arms and thus for himself by obtaining enough troops and supplies to accomplish his task. When he was rebuffed, and when it seemed that he was in imminent danger from a Confederate force he believed to be larger than his own, he began to feel frustrated and panicked. He had to do something, but what could he do?

Looking over the situation, the only thing he could do was to try to hide his weaknesses from the enemy. In California, newspapers had prevented him from keeping his bank problems quiet, so in Kentucky he believed that reporters would again publicize his deficiencies. He was not able to speed men and supplies to Kentucky nor wake his superiors to the seriousness of his needs, but he could, at least, prevent "newspaper spies" from making matters worse. In a key way, reporters became the personification of all Sherman's frustrations and, in acting against them, he was striking out against all his problems.

Sherman's attitude toward reporters was not necessarily irrational nor indicative of mental illness. He was not alone in his distrust of reporters; as is clear, other generals had similar sentiments. They and federal government officials were grappling with methods of control within and without the doctrine of freedom of the press. However, Sherman stood out in the force of his words and actions because of his psychic reaction to the stress of war and his personal worries.

Ironically, these same psychic reactions which made Sherman so thoroughly opposed to the press presented newspapers with the opportunity to strike back. What better way to get rid of an anti-press general than by capitalizing on his eccentricities and accusing him of insanity? What better way to discredit anti-press sentiments than by declaring a blatantly anti-press general insane? In attacking Sherman, newspapers were not only striking out at him, they were striking out at the concept of all government interference. Other government and military leaders felt the sting of barbed print, but the attack on a particularly vehement anti-press general was especially severe because his personal problems permitted it.

After the insanity charge had been widely circulated in the press and had been questioned only by family friend George D. Prentice's *Louisville Journal* (Sherman was "the equal of Richard the Lion Heart" in his "dauntless courage")[33] newspapers dropped the whole matter. Sherman's name disappeared from view almost as though newspapers hesitated to ruin their victory by overdoing their attack. The Sherman/Ewing family, however, was not so ready to forget.

The day after the insanity charge appeared in the *Commercial*, family troops mobilized to send a stinging rebuttal to the offending paper. They categorically denied every one of the original accusations. In two separate statements by his adjutant, General Halleck also defended his former subordinate against charges of insanity. "Far from being crazy," Halleck's adjutant wrote, Sherman "was employed in duties of the highest importance" to which he would return after his short rest.[34]

None of the newspapers which had reprinted the damning insanity charge now clipped the rebuttals. This was hardly objective journalism and it indicates that the press was not about to aid in refurbishing Sherman's reputation. The insanity charge against the anti-press general was left to stand unrebutted and therefore intact.

A split quickly developed among those supporting the harrassed general. His politician brother, John, and his former commander, Halleck, counselled no further action, urging that Sherman's future activities alone be allowed to rebut the accusations. The Ewings wanted to eradicate the stigma quickly by more immediate action. Sherman was torn between the two sides, but he was inclined to agree with his brother and with Halleck. He felt ashamed about his 23 December assignment to train recruits at Benton Barracks and wanted to be left alone. He gave vent to his feelings in his letters: he expressed fear he had disgraced his family; he felt guilty over not supporting his men well enough in Kentucky, particularly some Tennessee loyalists who had lost their lives on a bridge-burning mission for him; and he was distressed over having to fight former friends from the South. He was depressed and confused and even talked of taking a logistics position as a way of starting again.[35]

The Ewings would not let the matter drop. Sherman's wife, Ellen, undoubtedly with her father's approval, wrote a long letter to Abraham Lincoln, intimating that her husband's Kentucky problems were the result of some sort of an Army conspiracy against him. When the insanity charge had been published, she noted, he had received no official support. In all fairness, he should now be transferred back to the Eastern theater so he might have a chance to redeem himself.[36]

Lincoln did not answer the letter. Despite Sherman's opposition, Ellen decided to go to Washington and appeal to the president personally. On 20 January 1862 she and her father had an interview with Abraham Lincoln. The president listened carefully and praised Sherman, denying that he had ever thought him insane (although he had been concerned over the telegrams he had received from Kentucky). Ellen answered that her husband had never been insane and deserved to be vindicated from the deceit of Army generals and their newspaper cronies. Lincoln listened, but he made no promises, and the meeting ended inconclusively.[37] Yet he so charmed Ellen that she never blamed him for her husband's problems.

Many letters then passed between Sherman and his wife, but no further action was taken. Under Halleck's encouragement and with light duty, Sherman began to emerge from his depression. On 14 February 1862 Halleck was satisfied with his condition and returned him to a more active role in the war. Needing officers badly, Halleck made Sherman commander of the District of Cairo.[38]

This action satisfied Sherman and his brother, but not the Ewings. Ellen even believed that Halleck was part of a McClellan conspiracy against her husband. Despite the favorable turn of affairs, then, the Ewings hatched an elaborate plot to have the *Cincinnati Commercial* print a retraction of the insanity charge. The plan was to have Thomas Ewing, the family patriarch, write an editorial defending Sherman, then send it to Thomas Ewing Jr. in Washington. With the finished editorial in hand, Tom was to obtain publication permission for pertinent government documents buttressing it. He would then have these documents sent to Cincinnati as general news so that, when the editorial appeared, it would look as though it was based on the previously published documents. Ellen would then clip the editorial and send it to papers all over the country. This way, Sherman's name would be cleared, yet no one would guess the family's role in accomplishing it.[39]

The key to the plan's success was the *Commercial*'s

willingness to cooperate, but there was an immediate breakdown of communications. According to Thomas Ewing Jr., the *Commercial* agreed and then reneged on its promise, Editor Murat Halstead arguing that the public was just not interested in retractions of that sort. The Ewings, realizing that "a forced retraction would be of no value," dropped the whole idea.[40]

In later years, Editor Halstead had a different recollection of the episode. He said he had been shocked to learn from Thomas Ewing Jr. that Sherman was not crazy. This surprise had upset Ewing, Halstead remembered, but his offer to publish a retraction had had a calming effect. Halstead said he had counselled a statement from the Ewings rather than one from him, because he had felt theirs would carry more weight. He remembered no intricate plan nor any promises.[41]

Whatever the plan (later events indicated that Halstead's account was closer to the truth than the Ewing's) the family pressed ahead. In late March, Ellen and her father composed a statement and sent it to John Sherman and Thomas Ewing Jr. in Washington for correction and comment. Sherman, who had remained passive during all this family activity, now rebelled. When Thomas Ewing Jr. asked if Sherman wanted anything done for him in Washington, Sherman did not answer personally but had a staff officer write that he just wanted to be left alone.[42]

Sherman's disposition had obviously improved to the point that he could again declare his independence of the Ewings. As commander of the District of Cairo, he had witnessed Grant's successes at Forts Henry and Donelson, and soon after he became part of the successful general's advancing army. He became, in fact, a division commander in the newly created Department of the Mississippi. He was an integral part of a successful Union movement.

Unfortunately, this optimistic beginning nearly ended in disaster at Shiloh. On 6 April 1862 the Union forces were practically driven off the battlefield and were happy to regain their former positions the next day. Hurting the military even more, newspaper reporters published highly critical accounts of Union generalship. They accused the Union high command, particularly Grant, of negligence in allowing the advancing Confederates to surprise the Union Army. It is no exaggeration to say that newspapers were the main reason for this Union debacle becoming as controversial as it did. And as might have been predicted, Sherman was consequently in the center of the controversy.

Since Shiloh occurred near the beginning of the war, it was, in many ways, the result of the inexperience of soldiers and commanders on both sides of the battle line. It can also be argued that the extent of the controversy was the result of reporters' similar newness to their profession. Immediately after the battle, the few press reports were speculative rather than accurate. These reports were full of errors indicating that Union troops had driven off and routed the Confederate attackers. On 9 April news that an extended battle had taken place was published, but these accounts were again full of mistakes. On 10 and 11 April more accurate information was printed, but it was as yet not critical. As more news trickled in, however, the river of criticism began to rise. It reached flood stage on 14 April with the publication of one of the most famous Civil War news reports: Whitelaw Reid's sensational and damning criticism of the Union generalship at Shiloh.

Reid ("Agate") openly criticised the Union high command, particularly U. S. Grant, for not taking the necessary precautions against a Confederate attack. He called the Union positions inferior and condemned the wide gaps between units. No breastworks had been erected, and Union soldiers had not been prepared for the possibility of a Confederate advance. When the attack unexpectedly came early Sunday morning, the unprepared Union camps were a ghastly scene of confusion:

> Some, particularly among our officers, were not yet out of bed. Others were dressing, others washing, others cooking, a few eating their breakfasts. Many guns were unloaded, accoutrements lying pell-mell, ammunition was ill-supplied—in short the camps were virtually surprised—disgracefully, it might be added, unless some one can hereafter give some yet undetermined reason to the contrary—and were taken at almost every possible advantage.

Despite this negligence, Agate wrote, the Union Army had emerged victorious. But, poor Union generalship, particularly Grant's, had caused a host of unnecessary Union casualties.[43] Shiloh was a victory without cause for joy.

This article was not the first intimation of near-disaster at Shiloh, but it was the best written, it received the widest circulation, and it was the most openly critical attack of Union generalship. It caused newspaper emphasis, already changing, to shift completely from praise over a Union victory to open and hostile criticism of U. S. Grant and Union generalship. The boatloads of wounded making their way North and the long casualty lists appearing at the same time in the newspapers served only to dramatize and verify Agate's report.

Judging by Reid's earlier acceptance of the insanity charge against Sherman, a reasonable supposition is that Reid must have included Sherman in his attack on Union generalship at Shiloh. Sherman, after all, had chosen the Pittsburg Landing site, he had held the center of the Union line, his troops had been driven back, and in several instances they had broken and run before the Confederate charge. It would seem that he must certainly have been included among those generals found guilty of negligence.

Just the opposite occurred; Agate singled Sherman out for praise. He pictured him "Dashing along the line, encouraging them [his troops] everywhere by his presence, and exposing his own life with the same freedom with which he demanded their offer of theirs." His actions had been instrumental in preventing a complete rout. "Whatever . . . [might] be his faults or neglects," Agate wrote in apparent reference to Sherman's Kentucky tour, "no one . . . [could] accuse him of lack of gallantry and energy when the attack was made on his raw divisions."[44] Sherman was made the hero of Shiloh by a reporter who had previously helped build his insanity reputation. Sherman became a national celebrity because of his bravery and not because of his mental problems.

When the official battle reports of officers commanding at Shiloh were published, Sherman's reputation received another boost. His report became the most widely read and the most commented on, but it also became the most controversial. He factually presented his view of the fighting, contending that his troops had been ready when the attack had come and, except for several Ohio regiments, that they had fought well.[45]

Press reaction to this report was generally favorable. The *Cincinnati Commercial*, which just four months previously had initiated the insanity charge, now completely reversed its position. It praised Sherman's report as "the clearest, fullest and most authentic account of the great struggle on the Tennessee that has been written." Though Whitelaw Reid in the rival *Gazette* took a similar stance, the *Gazette* editorially disagreed. Probably reacting to the *Commercial*'s position, it denounced Sherman's report and exhumed the Kentucky controversy as part of its criticism. The *Louisville Journal* remained consistently favorable to Sherman and said Shiloh had elevated him "Proudly among the world's heroes."[46]

Sherman's performance at Shiloh, then, vastly improved his reputation. An unaccustomed wave of popularity swamped the insanity charge, and his spirits markedly lifted. "At last I stand redeemed from the vile slander of that Cincinnati paper," he exulted. He was doubly happy a month later when his brother wrote him that "All the absurd stories of the past were discredited by Shiloh."⁴⁷

One would think that Sherman's response to such praise would have been to enjoy the personal acclaim and ignore the criticism others received. But, this would have been out of character. His redemption from the insanity charge had not changed his view of reporters and newspapers. After briefly recognizing the refurbishment of his tarnished reputation, he expressed annoyance at the newspaper attacks on others, particularly his friend Grant. Feeling more confidence in himself and the Union cause, he lashed out against the press; he brusquely received his former confidant, Henry Villard, and told correspondent Albert D. Richardson that he hated newspapers and reporters because of their irresponsibility toward the truth. In private letters he was even more harsh. He called reporters "the most contemptible race of men that exist[ed], cowardly, cringing, hanging round, gathering their material out of the most pulluted sources." At Shiloh, they had ignored those who had fought and based their reports on the words of "cowardly rascals who ran away."⁴⁸

The Ewings reinforced Sherman's anger by writing him strong anti-press letters of their own. On 5 May 1862 they also took public action; they had the *Cincinnati Commercial* print a long defense of Sherman's conduct in Kentucky. Though the letter bore his signature, John Sherman was opposed to its publication and agreed to sign it only out of deference to the Ewings. The letter cited Sherman's "gallant conduct" at Shiloh as providing the proper occasion for discussing the "injustices" done him in Kentucky. His previous silence had been construed by some as giving assent to the insanity charge, but this was not true. It was obvious, the letter argued, that Sherman, far from being insane in Kentucky, had had a perceptive insight into problems there. Many of his suggestions (for example, press censorship) had been adopted and even his call for 200,000 men, seen in the context of the large forces now under arms, was obviously not crazy.[49]

The newspaper response was immediate. The *Commercial* and the *Louisville Journal* defended Sherman, while the *Cincinnati Gazette* was highly critical. Perhaps indicating more than it intended, the *Gazette* complained that military authorities had never properly evaluated Sherman's inferior Kentucky record because his family's influence had prevented it. Even his role at Shiloh had been marred by his complicity in the surprise. The *Commercial* disagreed completely, but it was the *Journal* that again expressed the strongest defense. Family friend George D. Prentice wrote: "Let Ohio editors endeavor to tarnish laurels nobly won. Kentucky admires him, loves him, feels the weight of obligation to him which can never be repaid."[50]

The *Commercial's* reversal was particularly dramatic but never explained unless one accepts at face value editor Halstead's earlier assertion that he was willing to right a wrong. More probably, Ewing pressure affected the change and the intracity rivalry with the *Gazette* should not be ignored in assessing both papers' responses to the controversy. Whatever the truth, the family was now content; even Ellen Sherman felt the *Commercial* seemed "disposed" to do her husband "justice." She was so pleased that, in phrases reminiscent of John Sherman's earlier counsel, she told her husband to show reporters "a little kindness," and they would prove his "best friends."[51]

Actually, the result was counterproductive; the letter reopened a controversy only recently overshadowed by Shiloh. It continued Sherman's feud with the press, especially the Cincinnati papers, and kept his name linked with controversy rather than glory. Coincidentally, the same day the defense appeared in the paper, Sherman was promoted to major general.

Again, Sherman was not satisfied. The insanity charge had been repudiated by the paper that had initiated it; other papers had reprinted favorable articles on his role at Shiloh; and his family's ill-timed defense had caused less damage than might have been expected. Still, he continued to lambast his journalistic adversaries. He called reporters "a set of dirty newspaper scribblers who have the impudence of Satan" and had caused the sectional split which had brought on the war. He warned that, if any reporter came into his camp, he would have him arrested "as a spy and . . . tried by a Court Martial and if possible shot or hung." He still believed reporters were a threat to Union arms, and nothing about Shiloh had changed his mind. Though he had been treated kindly, his friend Grant, whose ability he admired, had become so upset at the press accusations of drunkenness and incompetence, he had almost resigned. Sherman's support had helped change his mind, but the incident had once more convinced Sherman of the evil power reporters possessed.[52]

It was at this time too that another of Sherman's prejudices was reinforced. Despite his long acquaintance with politicians, including his father-in-law and his brother, Sherman distrusted holders of public office. The Lincoln adminstration had strengthened this feeling by its handling of the war effort and now the prejudice deepened because of Shiloh and the press controversy surrounding it.

Immediately after Shiloh, Benjamin Stanton, lieutenant governor of Ohio, had paid a visit to the battlefield. He had toured the site and had spoken to Ohio soldiers including Sherman. In late May, he published an attack on Generals Grant and Prentiss in his hometown paper in Bellefontaine, accusing these generals of culpability for the Union surprise. Sherman was not mentioned, but, with the advice and support of his wife and family, he took up the cudgels to defend his two colleagues. On 10 June 1862 he wrote Stanton a letter, later published, in which he defended Union generalship. In a very telling paragraph, he linked the lieutenant governor with his bitterest enemies, newspaper reporters.

> I am not surprised when anonymous scribblers write and publish falsehoods, or make criticism on matters which they know nothing or which they are incapable of comprehending. It is their trade. They live by it. Slander gives point and piquancy to a paragraph and the writer being irresponsible or beneath notice, escapes merited

punishment. It is different with men in high official station who like you descend to this dirty work.⁵³

Stanton responded, and the feud was on. Letters flew back and forth, and, at the behest of the Ewings, they were even published. Stanton quickly included Sherman in his list of incompetent generals, and these charges were considered important enough to have the military conduct an investigation. General S. A. Hurlbut, later one of Sherman's subordinates but at the time a division commander under Grant, investigated Stanton's accusations and reported they were false (hardly a surprising conclusion from a military man). Hurlbut even let Sherman write that part of the report which commented about Stanton that "sometimes scum of this sort issues to the top in times of agitation, and instead of being skimmed off and put off with other rubbish, dances out his hour of apparent vigor on the summit of popular effervescence."⁵⁴

The controversy remained a heated one and the combatants took it seriously, but it was virtually ignored by everyone else. In November when the last epistles changed hands, the press and public had long forgotten it, and Sherman was involved in other battles.

Stanton apparently became angry at Sherman because the general's report had named troops from the lieutenant governor's home town as among those who had run away during battle. Perhaps too, he decided to gain some political advantage from the dispute, or possibly he was still angry at having lost the 1860 senatorial nod to John Sherman.

Whatever the case, in 1865 he agreed to help promote a testimonial dinner for Sherman and admitted that he had been "clearly mistaken" in 1862.[55]

Sherman's reasoning is more pertinent to our interests. He saw his actions not only as a matter of loyalty to maligned friends, but also as a military necessity. In both his anti-press and his anti-Stanton position, he felt he was defending the Union cause. If politicians were allowed to attack soldiers with impunity, if newspaper reporters could print whatever they wished, victory in the war would be threatened.

This was, of course, not a new attitude for Sherman. He had felt this way before the war, during Bull Run, and in Kentucky. His reaction had always been to lash out, but there was a difference in his attitude after Shiloh. This battle restored his confidence in his own ability. He knew he could lead troops in combat (he no longer worried about his lack of Mexican War experience), and he knew that Union soldiers could hold their own against their Confederate counterparts. Supplies and manpower were becoming more plentiful, so the government seemed to be developing more responsibility. He no longer felt depressed about his future and that of the nation; victory was no longer the impossibility he had earlier feared. And if the Union won, his association with it in a position of authority would insure his own success.

There remained, of course, real obstacles to be overcome. The Confederate forces at Shiloh had shown themselves to be formidable, but Sherman had seen firsthand that they were not invincible. Politicians like Stanton were capable of mischief, but they could be handled. The press remained the real problem; reporters were information agents for the enemy and threats to security. There was still a need for censorship to prevent them from fulfilling their potentially harmful mission. In Kentucky he had feared he could not do enough to prevent reporter mischief, and, when the press had apparently bested him by publishing the insanity charge, he had despaired. Now as a result of his new confidence (ironically fostered by the press itself), he felt he could control reporters, or at least prevent them from dooming his cause. His anti-press attitude changed from one of despair to one of confidence. He now believed he could do what was necessary to keep reporters from publishing military secrets.

Newspapers had undergone a similar change. Shiloh had boosted the reporter's importance and showed that the press role in reporting the war was influential in forming northern opinion. Reporters had also become more confident and, like Sherman, they had gained needed experience at this battle. Their attitude toward him had also changed; his heroic conduct at Shiloh indicated he was far from insane. His anti-press activities might become a problem in the future, but reporters expressed little concern for the present because there was still no evidence to suggest he could effectively thwart them. Happily for Sherman and unhappily for reporters, Sherman's next assignment as military governor of Memphis, Tennessee, gave him the opportunity to try to put his anti-press beliefs into practice.

NOTES

1. William T. Sherman Diary, 2 April 1861, Sherman Family Papers, University of Notre Dame Archives. Hereafter cited as S. F. P., UNDA. WTS to John Sherman, 18 April 1861, William T. Sherman Papers, Library of Congress. Hereafter cited as: WTS Papers, LC.

2. WTS to Simon Cameron, 8 May 1861, WTS Papers, LC.

3. WTS Diary, 7, 11, 19, 21 June 1861 and Special Orders No. 105, Hq. of the Army, 20 June 1861, S. F. P., UNDA; WTS To Minnie Sherman, 14 July 1861, WTS Papers, Ohio Historical Society.

4. WTS to Ellen Sherman, 6 August 1861, S. F. P., UNDA; George B. McClellan, *McClellan's Own Story: The War for Union, The Soldiers Who Fought It, The Civilians Who Directed it and His Relation To It and to Them* (New York, 1887), pp. 69-70.

5. WTS to ES, 28 July, 15 August 1861, S. F. P., UNDA.

6. WTS, *Memoirs of General William T. Sherman* (New York, 1886), 1: 220–221; 15 August 1861 commission, S. F. P., UNDA.

7. R. M. Kelly, "Holding Kentucky for the Union," in *Battles and Leaders of the Civil War*, ed. Robert U. Johnson and C. C. Buel (New York, 1884-1888), 1: 381; James G. Randall, *Lincoln the President* (New York, 1945), 2: 3; *Louisville Journal*, 2 October 1861; Lowell H. Harrison, *The Civil War in Kentucky* (Lexington, 1975), pp. 15, 19; Harrison, "The Civil War in Kentucky: Some Persistent

takes complete responsibility for any ideas discussed in this chapter.

No previous historian has attempted a psychological evaluation of Sherman based on a thorough study of the sources. Several, however, have done so based on varying amounts of primary research. Otto Eisenschiml said Sherman "fell victim to war psychosis and fanaticism." Eisenschiml, "Sherman, Hero or War Criminal?" *Civil War Times Illustrated* 2 (January 1964): 29; T. Harry Williams wrote: "to put it in the mildest terms [Sherman suffered] a mental collapse." Williams, *McClellan, Sherman and Grant* (New Brunswick, N. J., 1962), pp. 56, 77; Stephen E. Ambrose disagreed with unnamed historians who, he said, have diagnosed Sherman as a manic depressive psychotic. (Indeed, one of the two psychiatrists Ambrose consulted characterized Sherman as a fully recovered manic depressive.) Ambrose said: "He was Sherman unique unto himself." "He was an intensely emotional man who had a highly developed imagination." Ambrose, "William T. Sherman: A Reappraisal," *American History Illustrated* 1 (January 1967): 6, 7; University of Pennsylvania Medical School Professor of Pathology Paul E. Steiner believes Sherman "had an anxiety state" in Kentucky "accompanied by a slight reduction in balance and poise but not in insight and touch with reality." He further argues that Sherman was worn out by cares and physical exhaustion. Unfortunately, Steiner's study is marred by his neglect of primary sources, numerous errors of fact and interpretation, and his identification with Sherman's likes and dislikes. His evaluation of Sherman's press battles, for example, concludes: "He [Sherman] has a secure place in history, they [reporters] live only for their infamy." Steiner, *Medical-Military Portraits of Union and Confederate Generals* (Philadelphia, 1968), pp. 54–55, 71–72, 96, 112. Albert

November 1861, S. F. P., UNDA; WTS to Halleck, 26, 27, 28 November 1861, Halleck to WTS, 27 November 1861, *O. R.*, Ser. I, 8: 379, 381-382, 391; Scuyler Hamilton to WTS, 28 November 1861, WTS Papers, LC; ES to WTS, 18, 20 November 1861, ES Diary, 26, 27 November 1861, S. F. P., UNDA; WTS, *Memoirs*, 1: 244; Special Orders No. 25, Hq., Dept. of Missouri, 2 December 1861, WTS Papers, LC; Halleck to McClellan, 2 December 1861, Ser. I, 7, pt. 2: 198; Jay Monaghan, *Civil War on the Western Border: 1854-1865* (Boston, 1955), p. 208.

28. ES Diary, 2, 4, 9, 10, 11 December 1861, S. F. P., UNDA: Maria Boyle Ewing to Thomas Ewing, Ewing Family Papers, Library of Congress. Hereafter cited as: E. F. P., LC. *New York Times*, n.d., enclosed in ES to JS, 10 December 1861, WTS Papers, LC; *Cincinnati Commercial*, 11 December 1861.

29. *New York Herald*, 19 December 1861; *Cincinnati Gazette*, 12, 13 December 1861; *Frank Leslie's Illustrated Newspaper*, 15 December 1861.

30. Villard, 1: 212–213; W. F. G. Shanks, "Recollections of W. T. Sherman," *Harper's New Monthly* 30 (April 1865): 644; E. V. Smalley, "Gen'l Sherman," *Century*, n.s. 5 (January 1884): 456; WTS to Halleck, 12 December 1861, WTS Papers, LC.

31. Murat Halstead, "Recollections and Letters of General Sherman," *Independent* 51 (15 June 1899): 1611-1612; Halstead, "Some Reminiscences of Mr. Villard," *American Review of Reviews* 23 (January 1901): 62; Villard, 1: 212–213.

32. This chapter, in an earlier form, was read and criticized by Dr. John Fleming, Chairman, Psychology Department, Gannon College and noted Erie, Pennsylvania, clinical psychologist, and by a prominent Erie, Pennsylvania, psychiatrist, who, for professional reasons, asked not to be cited by name. The author, of course,

D. Prentice and James Speed to Abraham Lincoln, 5 November 1861, Lincoln, *The Collected Writings of Abraham Lincoln*, ed. Roy P. Basler (New Brunswick, N. J., 1953), 5: 14–15n; D. C. Buell to H. W. Halleck, 3 January 1862, Buell, "William T. Sherman and the West," in *Battles and Leaders*, 1: 75; Thomas L. Connelly in his *Army of the Heartland: The Army of Tennessee 1861–1862* (Baton Rouge: Louisiana State University Press, 1967), pp. 62–77, castigates Albert Sidney Johnston's activities in Kentucky. He does, however, praise Johnston for his success in confusing Sherman and Buell as to the size of his forces. But, he says, Johnston also overestimated Sherman's strength.

22. *Chicago Tribune*, 5, 7 November 1861: *New York Times*, 11 November 1861; *Cincinnati Commercial*, 25 October 1861.

23. These telegrams are discussed in *McClellan's Own Story*, p. 201; WTS to ES, 23 October, 1 November 1861, S. F. P., UNDA; WTS to JS, 26 October 1861, WTS Papers, LC.

24. WTS to Lorenzo Thomas, 4, 6 November 1861, *O. R.*, Ser. I, 4: 332–333, 340–341; J. Whitelaw Reid, *Ohio in the War* (Columbus, 1893), 2: 430n; A. K. McClure, *Colonel Alexander K. McClure's Recollections of Half a Century* (Salem, Mass., 1902), pp. 332–333; Special Orders No. 305, Hq. of the Army, 13 November 1861, *O. R.*, Ser. I, 3: 570.

25. *New York Times*, 3 December 1861; *Cincinnati Commercial*, 9, 11, 16 November 1861.

26. WTS to JS, 4 January 1862, WTS Papers, LC; Captain Prince to Thomas Ewing, 8 November 1861, ES Diary, 8, 15 November 1861, ES to Maria Boyle Ewing, 11 November 1861, JS to WTS, 17 November 1861, S. F. P., UNDA.

27. Special Orders No. 8, Hq., Dept. of Missouri, 24

Questions," Kentucky State Historical Society *Register*, (January 1978), 3, 7–8.

8. Ibid., p. 7.

9. WTS Diary, 9, 19 September 1861, S. F. P., UNDA: WTS, *Memoirs*, 1: 222–224; WTS to ES, 18 September 1861, S. F. P., UNDA.

10. WTS to ES, 26 September 1861, ibid.

11. S. M. Bowman, "Major Gen. William T. Sherman," *United States Service Magazine* 2 (August 1864), 116–117; Kelly, 1:380–381; WTS to JS, 9 September, 5 October 1861, WTS Papers, LC.

12. *New York Times*, 2 October 1861.

13. WTS, *Memoirs*, 1: 227–228; General Orders No. 6, Hq., Department of the Cumberland, 8 October 1861, in *War of the Rebellion . . . Official Records of the Union and Confederate Armies* (Washington, 1880-1901), Ser. I, 4: 297. Hereafter cited as: *O. R.* Lloyd Lewis, *Sherman: Fighting Prophet* (New York, 1932), p. 188.

14. *Cincinnati Enquirer*, 5 November 1861.

15. WTS, *Memoirs*, 1: 227–228; Lewis, p. 191; WTS to ES, 12 October 1861, S. F. P., UNDA; WTS to Abraham Lincoln, 10, 14 October 1861, *O. R.*, Ser. I, 4: 300, 306–307.

16. WTS to ES, 12 October 1861, S. F. P., UNDA.

17. W. F. G. Shanks, *Personal Recollections of Distinguished Generals* (New York, 1866), pp. 54–55; Lewis, p. 185; Henry Villard, *Memoirs of Henry Villard: Journalist and Financier, 1835-1900* (Boston, 1904), 1: 210–211.

18. *Chicago Tribune*, 17 October 1861; *New York Times*, 16 October 1861; ES to WTS, 10 October 1861, S. F. P., UNDA.

19. Villard, 1: 211-212; Sherman, *Memoirs*, 1: 229–242.

20. *New York Tribune*, 30 October 1861.

21. *Cincinnati Commercial*, 13 November 1861; *New York Tribune*, 24 October 1861; James Guthrie, George

Castel says "Sherman lacked mental balance" and had "too much imagination." He was also inexperienced and had a "paradoxical mixture of ambition and pessimism." Castel, "The Life of a Rising Son," *Civil War Times Illustrated* 18 (July 1979), 45-46.

33. *Louisville Journal*, 17 December 1861.

34. P. B. Ewing to *Cincinnati Commercial*, 12 December 1861, in *Cincinnati Commercial*, *Cincinnati Gazette*, 13 December 1861, also found in *O. R.*, Ser. I, 52, pt. 1: 200–201; *St. Louis Missouri Democrat*, 13 December 1861; *New York Times*, 26 December 1861.

35. Halleck to ES, 14 December 1861, *O. R.*, Ser. I, 8: 441–442; JS to ES, 14 December 1861, S. F. P., UNDA; ES to WTS, 19, 20, 22 December 1861, TE to WTS, 22 December 1861, Hugh Ewing to WTS, 23 December 1861, S. F. P., UNDA; WTS to TE, 24 December 1861, E. F. P., LC; WTS to JS, 19 January 1862, WTS to JS, "Letters of Two Brothers: Passages from the Correspondence of General and Senator Sherman," ed. Rachel Ewing Sherman, *Century* 23 (January 1893): 427; WTS to JS, 12, 24 December 1861, WTS Papers, LC; WTS to ES, 1 January 1862, S. F. P., UNDA; WTS to W. K. Strong, 24 March 1862, *O. R.*, Ser I, 10, pt. 2: 65; WTS to ES, 11 January copy 19 January, 29 January 1862, S. F. P., UNDA.

36. ES to Abraham Lincoln, 10 January 1862, S. F. P., UNDA.

37. ES to WTS, 29 January, 4 February 1862, WTS to ES, 16 January 1862, copy, S. F. P., UNDA.

38. General Orders No. 37, Hq., Dept. of Missouri, 14 February 1862, *O. R.*, Ser. I, 8: 535.

39. JS to ES, 8 March 1862, ES to WTS, 12 March 1862, TE, Jr. to ES, 18 March 1862, ES to WTS, 21 March 1862, S. F. P., UNDA.

40. ES to "My Dear Brother," 25 March 1862, E. F. P., LC.

41. Murat Halstead to WTS, 16 March 1876, S. F. P., UNDA; Halstead, "Recollections," p. 1612.
42. ES to JS, ES to TE, Jr., 27 March 1862, L. M. Dayton to TE, Jr., 25 March 1862, E. F. P., LC.
43. *Cincinnati Gazette*, 14 April 1862.
44. Ibid. The authors of two modern histories of the Shiloh battle are critical of Sherman's performance in the engagement. Wiley Sword, *Shiloh, Bloody Shiloh* (New York, 1974) and James L. McDonough, *Shiloh—in Hell Before Night* (Knoxville, 1977).
45. Report of General William T. Sherman . . . , 10 April 1862, *O. R.*, Ser. I, 10: 248–254; Colonel Thomas Worthington, one of Sherman's regimental commanders criticized Sherman's conduct at Shiloh so severely that Sherman retaliated by court-martialling him. McDonough, p. 223.
46. *Cincinnati Commercial*, 15 May 1862; *Cincinnati Gazette*, 17 April 1862; *Louisville Journal*, 1, 6 May 1862.
47. WTS to ES, 14 April 1862, S. F. P., UNDA; JS to WTS, 19 May 1862, WTS Papers, LC.
48. Villard, 1: 273; Albert D. Richardson, *Secret Service: The Field, the Dungeon and the Escape* (Hartford, 1865), p. 248; WTS to TE, 27 April 1862, E. F. P., LC.
49. ES to WTS, 23 April 1862, S. F. P. UNDA; JS to *Cincinnati Commercial*, 30 April 1862, in *Cincinnati Commercial*, 5 May 1862.
50. *Cincinnati Gazette*, 6 May 1862; *Cincinnati Commercial*, *Louisville Journal*, 7 May 1862.
51. ES to WTS, 5 May 1862, S. F. P., UNDA.
52. ES to JS, 7 May 1862, WTS to JS, 12 May 1862, WTS Papers, LC; WTS to ES, 6 June 1862, WTS to Grant, copy, 6 June 1862, S. F. P., UNDA.
53. ES to WTS, 29 May, 1 June 1862, WTS to ES, 10 June 1862, S. F. P., UNDA; WTS to Benjamin Stanton, 10 June 1862, WTS Papers, LC, copy in S. F. P., UNDA.

54. Stanton to WTS, microfilm copy, 23 June 1862, WTS to Stanton, copy 12 July 1862, S. F. P., UNDA; TE to Stanton, 4 October, 1 November 1862, Stanton to TE, copy, 4 October 1862, WTS Papers, Ohio Historical Society; S. A. Hurlbut to J. A. Rawlins, 18 August 1862, *O. R.*, Ser. I, 10: 208–210; see WTS Papers, LC, for the Hurlbut report in Sherman's hand writing.

55. Stanton to H. H. Hunter, 16 January 1865, WTS Papers, LC.

4
The Czar of Memphis

THE THREE MONTHS after the repudiation of the insanity charge at Shiloh had been busy and successful ones for the revitalized Sherman. Union forces had captured the key railroad center at Corinth, Mississippi, and Sherman had also routed Confederate troops at nearby Holly Springs. The Union Army had recovered well from the Shiloh debacle and, under Halleck's plodding leadership, had advanced steadily. Instead of continuing to drive forward, however, Halleck divided his large force into several smaller ones and gave them various minor missions. The Union momentum was blunted not by Confederate troops but by a Union general's hesitation.

As part of this reorganization, Sherman was assigned to be military-governor of Memphis. Obviously he was no longer considered incompetent; otherwise he would not have been assigned such a difficult job. His task was to solidify the captured city in Union hands and receive and drill Union replacements. He seemed well suited for the task. His banking experience, his legal training, and his genuine affection for southerners seemed to have provided him with the necessary background and disposition for his job. His fiery temper, frustration with the sometimes slow workings of politicians and the democratic system, and his determination to let nothing stand in the way of Union success could be assets or drawbacks depending on how they motivated him.

Memphis had been in Union hands since early June of 1862. Before Sherman's arrival on 21 July 1862, five other military men (the most important being Grant) had commanded the city. So, whole series of regulations already existed. Still, Memphis had not recovered from the war it had seen; it was in a state of shock. The Civil War had proven hard on the whole state of Tennessee because of the state's split on the issue of secession. Tennessee belonged to the Confederacy, but a strong Unionist sentiment existed, particularly in the eastern part of the state. Even Mississippi River Memphis reflected this ambivalence; some Unionist sentiment was present even in this Confederate stronghold. Any person trying to govern this city would have to build up the Union elements at the expense of the more powerful Confederate majority.

The city's strong Confederate sentiment could be seen clearly in its press. Memphis newspapers were openly pro-Confederate, and their influence was wide. If not handled properly, they could provide the leadership around which opposition to Union authorities might gather.

The most influential Memphis paper was the one which was not even present in the city during the Union occupation. The *Memphis Appeal,* presses and all, had departed upon the June arrival of Union troops, continuing publication in Grenada, Mississippi, under its Memphis masthead. As the war progressed, it remained on the run just ahead of Union armies in a dramatic feat of journalistic boldness. It continued to publish newspapers as it ran, and these papers were read in Memphis. The *Appeal* was a source of much discomfort to Union authorities because there was no way to censor it short of capture.[1]

Other Memphis newspapers were unable to duplicate the *Appeal*'s daring dash and remained in the occupied city under strict Union control. Federal authorities monitored editorial content, changed one paper's name, and, for a short time, published another. The owner of the *Avalanche* was a staunch Confederate supporter, and he had left town when the Union troops had arrived. The word *Avalanche* was so closely associated with pro-Confederate sentiments that Federal officials renamed it the *Bulletin* after one of the papers it had recently absorbed. Military Governor Lew Wallace took over the *Argus,* another Memphis paper, and put it under the editorial control of Thomas W. Knox of the *New York Herald* and Albert D. Richardson of the *New York Tribune.* Although these two reporters were working for fiercely rival newspapers, before the war they had jointly published a newspaper in the West. They ran the *Argus* in Memphis for a month, after which it reverted to its previous editorial control.²

To try to offset the Confederate leanings of the *Appeal*, the *Avalanche*, and the *Argus*, Union authorities established their own paper just before Sherman's arrival, significantly named the *Union Appeal*. It was edited by a soldier, but lasted only a few months into Sherman's tenure. No information on its demise exists, but Sherman may well have suppressed it in anger over a specific article. He always believed too many officers kept reporters "in their employment to write them up in the newspapers," so even without any specific cause, Sherman would no doubt have suppressed the *Union Appeal* anyway. What need had he for a newly established house organ when he already controlled the existing papers in town? Besides, the fewer newspapers around, the better he liked it.³

When Sherman assumed command of Memphis in the middle of July, the status of a recently established military newspaper was not his biggest problem. From his temporary headquarters at the Gayoso House, he surveyed an economically depressed city. Many houses and businesses stood empty, the result of their owner's departure on the arrival of Union troops. Those stores still in operation were charging exorbitant prices for scarce commodities like fruits and vegetables. Social life was at a standstill; robbery and drunkenness were rampant. The Mississippi River town had never been a model of propriety, and the dislocation of the war had severely intensified its problems.⁴

Sherman quickly made clear his determination

to maintain control. He issued Unit Orders No. 56 which, in addition to announcing his arrival, reiterated all his predecessors' regulations. Included in these rules was the controversial loyalty oath first instituted by Grant during his tenure in the city. Anyone refusing to swear that he had not aided the Confederacy since the Union occupation of Memphis was to be exiled. Memphians had hoped that Sherman and his new administration would, at least, modify this oath, so they had delayed taking it. After Sherman's announcement, 400 persons jammed the Provost Marshal's office. Many more, however, left town, ignored it, or acquired false certification.[5]

Sherman took similarly strong action in other areas. Attending a church service, he noticed that the Episcopal priest omitted the standard prayer for the President of the United States, so he stood up and recited it himself in a loud voice. He wrote the city's mayor and told him that the city's government still existed and had the responsibility to correct municipal problems. If more police were needed, they should be hired and their expense borne by equitable taxation. He warned the mayor, however, that military affairs were the Army's sole prerogative. He left no doubt who was boss.[6]

He also laid down rules for the city's newspapers. He protested the *Union Appeal*'s publication of his life story because "Personalities in a newspaper ... [were] wrong and criminal." Besides, the account was full of errors. Similarly, he became angry over an article accusing an Army officer of wrongdoing. If the accusation was correct, the paper should have drawn up an indictment not published a story. He warned the paper and by extension the entire press under his jurisdiction:

> Use your influence to establish system, order, government. ... If I find the press of Memphis actuated by high principle and a sole devotion to their country, I will be your best friend; but, if I find them personal, abusive, dealing in innuendoes and hints at a blind venture, and looking to their own selfish aggrandizement and fame, then they better look out; for I regard such persons as greater enemies to their country and to mankind than the men, who, from a mistaken sense of State pride, have taken up their muskets.[7]

In no uncertain terms, therefore, Sherman told newspapers and their reporters that he would hold them strictly accountable for any news account he did not like. In his statement, he emphasized his opposition to personal attacks meant to increase newspaper circulation. He said nothing about military secrets. Obviously, the insanity charge was still fresh in his mind, and he was determined that no similar article would emanate from a press under his control. His statement that sensationalizing newspapers were a graver danger to the Union than Confederate soldiers shows how much his hatred for reporters had affected his common sense.

There was little the Memphis press could say or do in opposition to this blunt warning. But, northern newspapers with correspondents in Memphis were safely distant. Their reporters were not frightened and quickly forwarded critical reports. These accounts depicted Sherman as talking tough but being soft on secession. Northern newspaper articles protested the retention of the old city council and police, calling these individuals Confederate sympathizers. Sherman, they reported, even let a mill owner charge the military double rates for grinding corn despite the man's initial refusal to do anything for Union forces. Even worse, they complained, loyal Union men still had no influence in the city; Sherman was doing nothing to make their position more prominent, and this was "a blunder . . . without remedy and hence worse than a crime."[8]

Northern newspapers announced and commented on some new Sherman regulation or action each day. For example, Sherman ordered an end to the practice of paying specie for products coming from the Confederate States when Treasury notes were refused. He said that any person who refused payment in these notes was to be arrested and, if cotton was the commodity involved, half of it was to be confiscated. This was obviously an important statement both from an economic and a military government point of view, and newspapers recognized it as such. However, they disagreed as to its validity. The *Louisville Journal* was loyal as ever to Sherman, and the *St. Louis Missouri Democrat* also approved this regulation, but the *New York Tribune* and *Washington Star* felt it would cause more harm than good to the Union cause. Newspapers could not agree among themselves as to the correct policy, and such disagreement resulted in Sherman having as many defenders as he had opponents. His overall governance of Memphis, in fact, produced press ambivalence. An unnamed *New York Herald* reporter wrote: "If General Sherman's future course as commandment of Memphis is to be judged by his recent acts, the city under his administration will be ruled with an iron hand." Albert D. Richardson of the *New York Tribune*, on the other hand, told his readers: "(To characterize it very mildly) the eccentricities of his [Sherman's] administration . . . [are] working grievous injustice."[9]

Despite Sherman's strong bias against reporters and his persistent attempts to keep them away from his army, he was obviously not being successful. He was able to control newspapers published within his jurisdiction, but he could not censor correspondents of papers in the North. Memphis was not like an army camp, and correspondents were able to mingle with the populace and, if they wanted to, escape Sherman's notice. Sherman's surroundings hampered his press restrictions, and reporters were able to tell their readers in the North all about his activities. Since there was no fighting taking place, however, little of intelligence value was involved.

Sherman's administration of the city was going well, so press notice of him, even when critical, was mild. Nonetheless, he began to sink into depression. In August his wife was disheartened to have him write her of his belief he would die before the war was over. As if stimulated by this echo of Kentucky, she rejoiced over the fall from command of the man she blamed for her husband's problems there, George B. McClellan. Sherman answered with similar Kentucky allusions lamenting Lincoln's lack of insight in not agreeing with his call for a huge army. He recalled the insanity charge and scorned the "many flatterers" who now wished to make him a "prophet." Completing his return to the past, he wrote his daughter of his worries for his men and his unhappiness in fighting "old friends," even though they were now teaching their children to curse his name. He wished he could just remain in obscurity. Ellen responded as she had in Kentucky by urging him to come home or let her visit him there.[10]

As in Kentucky, Confederate sympathizers again surrounded Sherman and again he over-emphasized southern determination and southern strength. He concentrated on problems facing the Union forces and neglected to think of Federal advantages. He was once more in a position where slow decision making and often uncertain results had replaced the instancy of battle. In combat he had to act and had no time for recriminations and worries. In Memphis, he had to move slowly and he could seldom see any immediate results. He felt frustrated, uncertain, anxious, and depressed as he had in Kentucky. Yet, his reaction was not as severe. He showed few outward signs of discontent, and his management of Memphis continued to be efficient. He did not lose the confidence Shiloh had restored to him, and he did not now despair about Union arms as he had then.

In Memphis, reporters did not add to his frustrations as they had in Kentucky. Sherman now seemed able to act effectively against the press, and this may have provided a safety valve to prevent the build up of psychic problems. He was unable to impose a news blackout, but he had a firm hold on the local press. Northern newspapers were printing little of importance to the enemy, and their own inter-paper disagreements diffused even the mild censure of him they printed.

On several occasions, Sherman was even able to act directly against Northern newspapers and their reporters. The dispatch and relish with which he proceeded showed he had lost none of his anti-press prejudice and indicated his willingness to go as far as necessary to stymie reporters.

In early August Sherman received an order from U. S. Grant to arrest Warren P. Isham, the Memphis correspondent of the *Chicago Times*, and, incidentally, the brother-in-law of its editor, Wilbur F. Storey. Isham's transgression was an article "both false in fact and mischievous in character." Grant ordered Isham's imprisonment for the war's duration. Sherman quickly arrested the reporter, though neither he nor Grant ever made public a specific charge. Even his fellow reporters did not know the reason for his arrest. Correspondents for the *New York Tribune* and the *St. Louis Missouri Democrat* thought Isham might have been arrested because of a story he had written about ten ironclad ships allegedly running the blockade. But, they admitted, they were not sure. A later journalist related a spicier explanation in his book on Civil War reporters. He said Isham's arrest resulted from a story about a brigadier general, who, "in an advanced stage of undress," was caught at a disorderly house by the appearance of several Confederates. The general slipped out the window, and, in skimpy attire, ran to his camp where he told the guard a "harrowing tale of escape from spies and robbers." Isham discovered the truth, printed it, and was arrested "for giving aid and comfort to the enemy."[11]

Whatever the reason (and the bordello story must be highly seasoned with salt grains), Sherman arrested Isham with obvious delight. He countered the reporter's avowals of innocence by promising that Grant would release him if "the dishonest editor," who had substituted Isham's name to protect another, would now substitute himself in prison. Isham made no reply, and spent three months in an Illinois jail. Sherman was grateful for the chance to punish a reporter, because he "regard[ed] all these newspaper harpies as spies" and thought "they should be punished as such."[12]

A few weeks later, Sherman again took further anti-press action, this time against editor/publisher Samuel Sawyer of the *Union Appeal*, the Army newspaper in Memphis. General Samuel R. Curtis protested to Sherman about a 22 August article criticizing the behavior of Curtis and his troops in Clarendon, Arkansas. Sawyer argued that a chaplain in Lew Wallace's forces had written the article and the minister, not Sawyer, should be punished. Sherman rejected the plea, ordered Sawyer arrested for "false and libelous publication," and set bail at $1,000.[13] Whether Sawyer or the chaplain ever received any further punishment is unknown, but perhaps this was the occasion for the demise of the *Union Appeal* mentioned above.

Sherman showed clearly in both these incidents how far he was willing to go in his battle with reporters. In the Isham case, the correspondent may have been arrested for providing intelligence to the enemy, but this is uncertain because the charge was never made public (an ominous circumstance in itself). In the Sawyer case, no such doubt exists. Sherman arrested a newspaper man simply because he and a subordinate did not like a specific article. Publication of vital military secrets was not the issue. Sherman censored the press because he disapproved of an article critical of the conduct of Union soldiers. This was a clear violation of the First Amendment whether in peace or war. The Founding Fathers had framed the First Amendment precisely to protect the press' right to be critical. The framers realized that once criticism was banned, the press would no longer be independent and would then only be able to publish what those in power permitted. But, Sherman wanted just that; he wanted civilian and military leaders not simply to regulate newspapers but to suppress them completely. Later, he would admit this openly and even take stronger action to insure it, but this attitude was already clear here.

In his defense, Sherman argued that, in war, the Constitution had to be set aside.[14] Any criticism of the war, he said, aided the enemy. A newsman helped the Confederate cause not only by printing intelligence but also by criticizing the Army and its leaders and thereby lowering military and public morale. He believed any information about Union troops might be of value to the enemy, so it made sense, he argued, to prevent even the most minute fact or miniscule criticism from appearing in print. Sherman believed the military had to maintain total secrecy, and, consequently, the First Amendment was invalid in wartime.

If Sherman needed further support for his anti-press position, he received it in dramatic form in Memphis. He discovered that letters and newspapers were being exchanged between Memphis and the Confederate Army through a series of drop points such as homes, railroad culverts, and even a rotten tree. His own spy network indicated that northern newspapers were indeed received regularly in Confederate areas. This discovery of Confederate determination to read northern papers only convinced him again how right he had always been. The Confederates considered northern newspapers valuable; therefore these papers had to be suppressed. Otherwise, the Confederates would receive important information about Union forces.[15]

Consequently, Sherman continued to monitor newspapers and to punish them whenever he saw something he did not like. Again he displayed his disregard for newspaper rights. In the fall of 1862, he found the *Argus* guilty "of showing a tendency, in the general tone of the paper, inimical to the interests of the United States and foster[ing] a spirit of insubordination and resistance to authority." The *Argus* editors were hauled before the Provost Marshal and required to take out a $10,000 bond as a guarantee of future virtue. Despite this obvious example of what later generations would call "prior restraint," other newspapers remained silent about his restriction of a fellow journalist. Only the *Appeal*, safely distant from Sherman's intimidation, responded. It also gratuitously attacked Memphis papers for their timidity in not joining in the protests.[16] Distance was a marvelous spur to courage. Northern papers, also safely distant from the general's wrath, continued publishing comments on his various activities, but they did not criticize his treatment of their journalistic brethren in Memphis. Sherman's anti-press activity produced little criticism in northern newspapers. Yankee editors either saw Sherman's rough handling of Memphis newspapers as only appropriate for Rebel newsmen or they did not realize that what he did in Memphis he felt should be done throughout the North. As long as northern newspapers were not directly affected, they apparently were not concerned. Personal not constitutional considerations obviously motivated their activities.

Sherman's activities that received the most northern press coverage concerned liquor and slavery. Sherman felt that alcohol, along with prostitution, was a private matter and out of his jurisdiction. He did nothing to hinder the thriving bordellos, and he reopened saloons to stimulate business and tax revenue. Northern newspapers were silent on his prostitution stand, but they criticized his liquor regulation. The *Cincinnati Gazette* called the order dangerous to public welfare because it had caused drunkenness, shootings, and "a hell of social errors." A *St. Louis Missouri Democrat* reporter disagreed with the revenue justification, arguing that the saloons' reopening had increased disorder. This mayhem necessitated more police, which meant the need for more revenue, consequently more saloons to gain additional monies. But, more saloons meant more disorder, more police, *ad infinitum*. Citizens, he said, would happily pay a liquor tax by "subscription," if Sherman would close the saloons and end the vicious cycle. Sherman responded with an order threatening to demolish disorderly saloons, and the problem lessened. At least, newspapers did not mention it again.[17]

The press also commented on Sherman's 8 August 1862 policy governing the area's slaves. In this regulation, he said it was "neither his duty nor pleasure to disturb the relation of master and slave"; this was a legal problem. Until the judicial systm began functioning efficiently again, however, he decreed that loyal slaveowners would recover their slaves, disloyal ones would lose them. Perhaps Sherman's pronouncement was influenced by the Congressional Confiscation Act of 17 July, although his statement was much less thorough and harsh. Interestingly, too, Sherman's regulation predated Lincoln's 22 September Emancipation Proclamation and, like it, viewed slavery from a strictly wartime perspective. Like Lincoln, Sherman handled the explosive issue carefully, but, unlike the president, his views on slavery never grew. In fact, he even felt Lincoln's statement was too radical.[18]

The northern press regarded Sherman's slavery proclamation with favor. As the *St. Louis Missouri Democrat* put it: "everybody, even slaveholders, wonder[ed] that it was not done before." No Memphis paper offered any opposition to Sherman's statement, but the *Memphis Bulletin* opposed Lincoln's proclamation. For several days after the proclamation's promulgation, the *Bulletin* clipped and published a whole series of northern press criticisms.[19] Since Sherman also disagreed with Lincoln's pronouncement, the *Bulletin* went unpunished. Despite his repeated protestations that any criticism of the war effort gave aid and comfort to the enemy, Sherman did nothing to suppress criticism when it agreed with his own. Though he would not admit it, Sherman's anti-press attitude was based on personal biases rather than adhering to any contemporary civil or military interpretation of the Constitution or adopting a cogent philosophy of putting the constitution aside during war.

This attitude could also be seen in Sherman's reaction to criticism of another one of his Memphis actions. He expended much writing paper defending his opposition to the United States Sanitary Commission on the grounds that it disrupted Army efficiency. He compared its propensity for mischief to that perpetrated by the press. Soldiers, he argued, needed discipline not coddling. The Army was becoming too democratic as soldiers attempted to control their superiors by complaining to the press that these officers excluded the Commission. If the military was to achieve success, such behavior had to be stopped. Military men could only speak the truth if it was "palatable to the crowd," while their attackers were "allowed the wildest liberty and license." He would not allow himself to be so intimidated. He would "be governed by the 'Law and the regularly constituted authorities' and not by the Press."[20] In short, newspapers were responsible for his problems with the Sanitary Commission; reporters were behind every problem. Strong measures against them were essential, if he was to be free of criticism over this and other issues.

Clearly then, Sherman held that press criticism when directed against him was detrimental to the war effort, yet he was free to criticize this same war effort as much as he wished. If press criticism agreed with his views, it was permissible; if not, it was a threat to national security. Sherman made himself the sole definer of responsible journalism and the First Amendment.

Sherman was receiving little criticism from reporters during the early fall of 1862. All was going well in Memphis, and on 24 September 1862 he gained control of one of the four divisions of Grant's newly organized District of West Tennessee. His headquarters remained in Memphis, but his days were even more crammed with activity than ever before. The return to action and the continuing confidence that he had matters under control caused his depression to lift. Generally he rose before day break and kept busy all day, seven days a week. In November, he received a welcome break when his wife and children came for a visit and witnessed fifteen officers present him with a sword for bravery at Shiloh. Ellen Sherman proudly watched her husband being feted and commented that "All the newspaper compliments in the world would have failed to gratify . . . [him] half as much as this evidence of attachment and confidence on the part of his tried and valued officers."[21] Even on a day of celebration, newspapers and reporters were never out of mind.

By October the tempo of fighting had increased,

and press coverage of Sherman's Memphis activities lessened. Only the *New York Herald* with its large staff had enough reporters to continue to be able to publish reports from the Bluff City. Other papers sent their limited number of correspondents into the field to report on the renewed fighting. As a result, the *Herald* published the only extensive information on Sherman, and these reports were favorable. The *Herald* exaggeratedly announced that Sherman's efforts had converted enough people in the Memphis area "to start a Union club in a prominent place in North Mississippi." While this statement is debatable, Sherman, without question, was doing a good job in Memphis. Economic life had improved, and the city was secure. Sherman felt so militarily confident that, when a Confederate general threatened to take the city in sixty days, Sherman sent him a bottle of whiskey and invited him to try.[22] Such a reply would have been impossible earlier in the war, and it demonstrates how much Sherman's confidence and self-esteem had grown since the dark days of Kentucky and Missouri.

In late November, Sherman was assigned a combat task; he was ordered to attack the region north of Vicksburg as part of a three-pronged movement against that Mississippi Gibraltar. He gave up his Memphis command. His departure occasioned a *New York Herald* lament, and a Memphian thanked him on behalf, he said, of all citizens.[23] The Memphis press let him depart quietly. Sherman had warned them on his arrival that he was against newspaper personality sketches and personal praise, so Memphis papers apparently took him at his word and said nothing.

In Memphis, Sherman had demonstrated that he could be a successful administrator despite strain and depression. Unlike his Kentucky experience, he had enough power in Memphis to act against deficiencies. He could also see that while the Federal situation remained difficult it was hardly hopeless. Consequently, he did not again despair. He possessed enough confidence in himself and in the Union war effort to avoid becoming obsessed with the possibility of inevitable disaster. He realized the Union cause looked bright, and he could have a vital part in any victory. His hoped-for success seemed on the verge of accomplishment.

Since he believed so firmly that reporters and their papers were stumbling blocks to his and the Union's success, his suppression of journalists in Memphis helps account for his more confident disposition. He saw firsthand that he could effectively censor the press under his jurisdiction. Even the distant newspapers could be restrained by specific actions against their reporters on the spot. It did not concern him that such action violated reporters' rights to gather news and the nation's right to know. He did not realize that his definition of contraband news was based less on war necessity or constitutional philosophy than on concern for personal reputation. In Memphis, Sherman displayed the pervasiveness of his anti-press bias and his willingness, given the power and opportunity, to violate the Bill of Rights. He now contended openly that newspapers under his jurisdiction could print only what he considered to be proper. Anything else, he argued, threatened Union arms, and he was obligated to suppress it.

Despite Sherman's resolution and his military power, he was unable to silence the press totally. Newspaper activity, some of it critical, continued, but it was subdued. Sherman's threats and his anti-press actions undoubtedly influenced newspapers to refrain from too much comment. Reporters were able to file stories despite his animosity, so why rankle him unnecessarily by debating his restrictions. Reporters were not pleased with their situation, nor had they developed any love for their unbending foe. His performance at Shiloh and his efficient administration in Memphis showed them he was not mad, but his anti-press activities also confirmed that he was no reporters' friend either. Sherman's actions ingrained in reporters how determined a foe he was and how careful they would have to be in his jurisdiction. But it was difficult to argue with success, and so long as Sherman was successful and so long as correspondents were able to publish their reports, they could ignore his biases and obstructionism.

Ominously, this situation could change very quickly. Should Sherman more effectively suppress reporters, and/or should correspondents print more offensive material, the battle between the general and the reporters would escalate again. Now both seemed content; such feelings, however, were not permanent.

NOTES

1. Thomas H. Baker, *The Memphis Commercial Appeal* (Baton Rouge, 1971), pp. 93–112.
2. Ibid., pp. 94–95; Joseph H. Parks, "Memphis Under Military Rule, 1862–1865," (East Tennessee Historical Society) *Publications* 14 (1942): 34; Lew Wallace to Editor of *Memphis Argus*, 17 June 1862, quoted in Thomas W. Knox, *Campfire and Cottonfield* (New York, 1865), p. 190; *New York Herald*, 21 June 1862; J. Cutler Andrews, *The North Reports the Civil War* (Pittsburgh, 1953), p. 251.
3. Baker, p. 95; Parks, p. 34; William T. Sherman to P. P. L. Hommedieu, 7 July 1862, William T. Sherman Papers, Library of Congress. Hereafter cited as: WTS Papers, LC. *Memphis Appeal*, 9 September 1862.
4. *Memphis Bulletin*, 23, 28 July 1862; *Memphis Appeal*, 25 July 1862.
5. Unit Orders No. 56, Hq., 5th Division, Army of the Tennessee, 21 July 1862, *War of the Rebellion . . . Official Records of the Union and Confederate Armies* (Washington, 1880-1901), Ser I, 17, pt. 2: 110. Hereafter cited as: O. R. *New York Herald*, *New York Times*, *Louisville Journal*, *Washington Star*, 26 July 1862; Parks, pp. 35-38; *Memphis Bulletin*, 22, 23 July 1862.
6. Lloyd Lewis, *Sherman: Fighting Prophet* (New York, 1932), p. 243; Parks, pp. 38-39; Robert J. Futrell, "Federal Military Government in the South, 1861–1865," *Military Affairs* 15 (Winter 1951): 184–185.
7. WTS to Samuel Sawyer, 24 July 1862, *O. R.*, Ser. I, 17, pt. 2: 116–117; WTS to Editors of *Bulletin* and *Appeal*, 21 August 1862, Sherman Family Papers, University of Notre Dame Archives. Hereafter cited as: S. F. P., UNDA. The August letter warned against anonymous articles and urged opposition to guerrillas.
8. *Cincinnati Commercial*, 28, 30 July 1862; *St. Louis*

Missouri Democrat, 28, 29 July 1862; *Chicago Tribune*, 30 July 1862; *New York World*, n.d., WTS Papers, LC; *New York Herald*, 15 August 1862.

9. *Louisville Journal*, 30 July 1862; *St. Louis, Missouri Democrat*, 2 August 1862; *New York Tribune*, 31 July, 1 August 1862; *Washington Star*, 5 August 1862; *New York Herald*, 4 August 1862; *New York Tribune*, 6 August 1862.

10. Ellen Sherman to WTS, 6, 9 August 1862, WTS to ES, 10 August 1862, S. F. P., UNDA; WTS to Minnie Sherman, 16 August 1862, WTS, "My Father's Letters," ed. Minnie Ewing Sherman, *Cosmopolitan* 12 (November 1891), 67; WTS to ?, 17 August 1862, ES to WTS, 17 August 1862, S. F. P., UNDA.

11. Grant to WTS, 8 August 1862, quoted in Sylvanus Cadwallader, *Three Years With Grant*, ed. Benjamin P. Thomas (New York, 1956), p. 3; *St. Louis Missouri Democrat*, 19 August 1862; *New York Tribune*, 21 August 1862; Emmet Crozier, *Yankee Reporters: 1861-1865* (New York, 1956), pp. 319-320; Historian Justin Walsh states that the bordello story was printed in April and Isham was arrested in August for a purely fictitious story of rebel ironclads at Pensacola, Florida. Walsh, *To Print the News and Raise Hell: A Biography of Wilbur F. Storey* (Chapel Hill: University of North Carolina Press, 1968), pp. 176–179.

12. WTS to Grant, 17 August 1862, *O. R.*, Ser. I, 17, pt. 2: 178.

13. *New York Tribune*, 5 September 1862.

14. See p. 9.

15. Court-martial of Thomas W. Knox, Records of the Office of Judge Advocate General (Army), Record Group 153, LL 554, pp. 28-29, National Archives and Records Service, Washington.

16. *Memphis Bulletin*, 8 November 1862; *Memphis Appeal*, 21 October 1862.

17. *Cincinnati Gazette*, 18 August 1862; *St. Louis Missouri Democrat*, 19 August 1862; *Cincinnati Commercial*, 26 August 1862; Special Orders No. 180, mentioned in *Chicago Tribune*, 21, 23 August 1862.
18. General Orders No. 67, Hq., 5th Division, Army of the Tennessee, 8 August 1862, *O. R.*, Ser. I, 17, pt. 2: 158-160; for Sherman's attitudes towards blacks, see p. 168 in this book; see also Robert K. Murray, "Sherman, Slavery and the South," masters thesis, Ohio State University, 1947, and Murray, "General Sherman, the Negro and Slavery: The Story of an Unreconstructed Rebel," *Negro History Bulletin* 22 (March 1959): 125-130, and Kathleen M. Cresto, "Sherman and Slavery," *Civil War Times Illustrated* 17 (November 1978): 13–21.
19. *St. Louis Missouri Democrat*, 14 August 1862; *Memphis Bulletin*, 1, 2, 3 October 1862.
20. WTS to Grant, 26 August 1862, quoted in WTS, *Memoirs of William T. Sherman* (New York, 1886), 1: 302; WTS to John Sherman, 26 August 1862, 22 September 1862, WTS Papers, LC; WTS to W. W. H. Taylor, 25 August 1862, *O. R.*, Ser. I, 52, pt. 1: 275-276.
21. General Orders No. 83, Hq., Dept. of West Tennessee, 24 September 1862, *O. R.*, I, 17, pt. 2: 237; WTS to ES, 4 October 1862, ES to Thomas Ewing, 6 November 1862, S. F. P., UNDA; the citation presented with the sword is preserved in the WTS Papers, LC.
22. *New York Herald*, 20, 25 October 1862. Historian Ralph H. Gabriel concluded that Sherman's Memphis activities were "an example of an efficient and humane management of a local area." Gabriel, "American Experience with Military Government," *American Historical Review* 49 (July 1944): 637.
23. *New York Herald*, 26 December 1862; Hoteq [sic] to WTS, 1 December 1862, WTS Papers, LC.

5
The Press on Trial

UNION ACTIVITY in the early years of the war had resulted in conspicuous failures in the Virginia theater. In the West, however, the opposite had occurred; Northern arms had been so successful that almost the entire Mississippi River was in Union hands by the end of 1862. There was only one Confederate stronghold left preventing total Federal control: Vicksburg, Mississippi, high on bluffs overlooking the river.

On 8 December 1862 William T. Sherman and U. S. Grant met at Oxford, Mississippi, to plan a three-pronged attack to overwhelm the Mississippi Gibraltar. Grant, Sherman, and New Orleans-based Nathaniel Banks were to make a coordinated drive against Vicksburg with Sherman's forces to strike Chickasaw Bayou, the anchor of the Confederate right. The plan proved to be a failure. Grant's supply lines were cut, and he was unable to attack Vicksburg from the East. Banks's illness prevented his attack from the South, and Sherman was soundly repulsed on 29 December when unknowingly he made what turned out to be a solo assault.¹

Prior to his expedition's embarkation, Sherman had been in an excellent frame of mind. He was particularly happy to be associated with Grant, a man he had come to admire and respect. He was determined all would go well and, as part of his preparations, he issued an anti-press directive. General Orders No. 8 forbade any civilians but the transports' crews from accompanying the expedition. Punishment was set at conscription into the Army and then work as a deck hand, if the accused party persisted in his misbehavior. Anyone on board the transports who wrote anything for publication would be arrested and treated as a spy.²

This regulation was an obvious extension of the ideas Sherman had developed in Memphis. If his expedition was to be a success, the press had to be censored. What better way to censor reporters than by completely excluding them. No news could reach the enemy if there was no one present to write it up and see that it was published. Exclusion was the complete, the perfect censorship. It was prior restraint of the highest order.

At first, reporters did not take Sherman seriously; several even tried to get special exemptions. When they were firmly rebuffed, they realized he meant business. But they did not panic. They too had learned from their Memphis experience and believed that, despite Sherman's order, they could skirt his restrictions and get the news. The *New York Tribune*'s "Gualbert" said he was not surprised at the order and confidently predicted that, regulation or not, "there will be correspondence from the expedition." Junius H. Browne of the same paper said Sherman had issued the order because he blamed reporters for "his reputation for occasional insanity." Browne said Sherman would not have had such a reputation "without some very satisfactory cooperation on his part." Actually, Sherman was "a competent and an efficient officer," Browne concluded, but, as this "absurd order" showed, he had "sundry defects of judgment."[3]

Reporters' unconcern proved to be accurate; a number of correspondents were able to attach themselves to the Sherman expedition, and reports of the Vicksburg battle reached the northern papers. Sherman quickly learned of the correspondents' presence and issued a second order directing them to be sent to the front to "pass powder." Like the first, this order was ignored, and Sherman was stuck with his journalistic impedimenta.[4]

During the battle, reporters suffered with the troops because of the mud and rain. Several were nearly captured, and their early reports mirrored the confusion of the Chickasaw Bayou failure. The first accounts of the 29 December encounter appeared on 6 January 1863 and erroneously announced the capture not only of the Bayou but of Vicksburg itself. Secretary of State William H. Seward, surveying the press accounts, disgustedly complained of their "confused and unsatisfactory" nature. It was not until 12 January that the truth came out; it was then reported that "General Sherman's repulse was complete."[5]

In their confusion, reporters had groped for the

truth, but had found only part of it. They were unaware of the failure of the three-pronged plan and thus placed full blame for the debacle on Sherman. Even the consistently friendly *Louisville Journal* joined in, clipping a *St. Louis Missouri Republican* article accusing Sherman of underestimating the enemy and displaying "a lamentable ignorance of the character and extent of their defences." The *Chicago Tribune*, though at first an advocate of moderation and objectivity, headlined a Vicksburg report: "A Fredricksburg in the West! Another National humiliation? More Blundering! Immense energy squandered! Heroism thrown away! Defeated, baffled, repulsed, disheartened!" It then called for Sherman's dismissal and described him as "most bitterly hated." There was no hope for Vicksburg's capture, it concluded, until he was replaced.[6]

Other papers joined in, and press criticism of Sherman's battle performance was quickly mingled with attacks on his anti-press activities. His failure in battle was combined with accusations of his searching through mailbags and confiscating correspondents' reports. The *Cincinnati Gazette* asked why he feared the truth.[7]

The attacks quickly became vicious, and the insanity charge, thought to be discredited by Shiloh and Memphis, was resurrected. The *Louisville Journal*, quoting the *St. Louis Missouri Democrat*, the newspaper identified with the powerful Francis Preston Blair family (one of whose sons was a general in Sherman's command), reported a "reckless disregard of common prudence on the part of General Sherman and his advisers." A "prudent general" would have foreseen defeat in the Vicksburg circumstances. Franc B. Wilkie, "Galway" of the *New York Times*, said everyone could "see the madness of Gen. Sherman" in his choice of attack sites. Obviously unaware of Grant's and Banks's failure to aid Sherman, a *Times* editorial concluded: "Sherman, who, during the war, has suffered an amazing variety of ups and downs, was anxious to reduce the great stronghold by his own unaided efforts. Hence the insane attack." The *Cincinnati Gazette* took the final step. It quoted the *Jackson* (Miss.) *Appeal* (actually the *Memphis Appeal* then being published in Jackson) that Sherman was "confined to his state room perfectly insane."[8] Sherman's failure at Vicksburg provided the opportunity for the press to accuse him once more of insanity. Reporters combined his military and his anti-press activities, showing clearly that their criticisms were caused as much by one as by the other.

Nowhere was this linkage more evident than in the *New York Times* columns of Franc B. Wilkie. In a 1 January 1863 dispatch, not published until 18 January due to Sherman's mail interference, Wilkie made this point clearly. "Had the commanding General W. T. Sherman and his Staff, spent half the time and enterprise in the legitimate operations of their present undertaking, that they have in bullying correspondents, overhauling mailbags and prying into private correspondence, the country would not now have the shame of knowing that we have lately experienced one of the greatest and most disgraceful defeats of the war." The next day, Wilkie supplied the *coup de grace*. He accused Sherman of being "carried away by jealousy of other commanders." He had "insane ambition."[9]

Wilkie did not limit his criticism to the commanding general alone; he also attacked, by name, Sherman's adjutant, Colonel J. H. Hammond. Since an adjutant's task is to serve as his commander's right arm, Wilkie's criticism of Hammond was an extension of his attack on Sherman. Hammond's reaction likewise reflected Sherman's attitude.

In castigating Hammond, Wilkie again linked military failure with anti-press activities. He called Hammond "a man whose aptitude for sneaking, blusters and insult . . . [qualified] him admirably for some business in which crawling under beds, listening at key-holes and eavesdropping generally . . . [were] the main peculiarities." "Sherman's gallantry in storming the heights above Chickasaw Bayou was only equalled by the gallantry of Hammond in his assault upon the mailbags." "Sherman's failure," Wilkie ridiculed, was "counterbalanced by the success of Hammond."[10]

The Adjutant's reaction closely resembled Sherman's earlier comments against reporters. There was only one minor difference. Sherman always talked of hanging reporters; Hammond threatened to shoot Wilkie. The reporter became justifiably frightened and asked a friend for help. He waited on board the transport, *City of Madison*, for this friend, Captain, later Colonel, Charles Morton, to secure him a pistol. Just then, Hammond entered the room. According to one account, Hammond "glared . . . with what seemed a diabolical expression, and a murderous look appeared to fill his eyes." Fortunately, a visibly shaken Wilkie remembered, Hammond turned and left immediately. In another account, Wilkie quoted a letter written by Colonel Morton some twenty-five years after the event. This account was even more dramatic. Morton said: "Among other things Hammond intimated that you were not a descendent of Adam, but that your origin might be determined on the Darwinian theory. He also insisted in most vigorous language that you rivalled Ananias of ancient fame [a notorious liar in the Bible]. I remember that much of the profanity was original, and, as I then was a youngster, it was highly appreciated." Wilkie, Morton remembered, challenged Hammond to a duel, but an accord was reached through his mediation.[11]

The accuracy of these stories is perhaps not as important as the incident itself. Relations between reporters and military officers had indeed reached a low point when there were threats of shootings and fears for life. Sherman's anti-press attitude allowed a situation of the worst magnitude to develop. Had Hammond actually shot Wilkie, his inspiration, to an important degree, would have been Sherman's rhetoric. Violence or the threat of violence is the most ominous kind of censorship, and Sherman's attitude not only tolerated but actually encouraged it.

Wilkie was not alone in his strongly worded linkage of battle failure and anti-press success. Thomas W. Knox of the *New York Herald* wrote a scathing criticism of the Vicksburg failure which became the most controversial description of the affair. With studied sarcasm, Knox wished Sherman and his staff had acted with as much energy against the enemy as they had against reporters. Then, Sherman would have been as successful against the Confederates as he had been against Knox's and other correspondents' mailed reports. But, if the general felt he needed Knox's letter to compose his battle report, he was welcome to it. Sherman was guilty of mismanagement, Knox continued, and he was now trying to prevent the North from learning about it. As part of the cover-up, he was even sending hospital boats away despite the agony this caused to his wounded men. "Insanity and inefficiency have brought their result: let us have them no more. With another brain than that of General Sherman's, we will drop this disappointment at our reverse, and feel certain of victory in the future."[12]

Wilkie's statement about Sherman's insane jealousy and Knox's comment about "another brain" were obvious references to another complicating factor in the Vicksburg affair. After the battle was over, Sherman was replaced as commander of the expeditionary force by Major General John McClernand. Seeing this occur, the press decided that Sherman had made his solo attack on Chickasaw Bayou in order to try to forestall the change. Newsmen were unaware that McClernand, a leading Illinois politician and highly successful troop recruiter, was receiving the command not because of any Sherman deficiencies but because Lincoln needed his continued support in the important Midwest. McClernand would have replaced Sherman no matter what had happened at

Vicksburg. His arrival under the best of circumstances would have caused problems, but his arrival at this point only made matters worse. Grant and other West Pointers distrusted all political generals while Sherman took the change personally.

The press did not understand these subcurrents and simplistically equated Sherman's solo attack with the coming of McClernand. When the Illinois politician took command of the Vicksburg expeditionary force and captured Arkansas Post, utilizing plans already set in motion by Sherman, press confusion increased. Which general should receive credit for the victory, Sherman or McClernand? Most papers chose McClernand. Only the *Cincinnati Commercial*, now apparently fully converted to Sherman's cause, defended him. He should get the credit for Arkansas Post because the plan was his. The *Commercial* conceded that Sherman was "abrupt, haughty, and at times dogmatical, easily irritated and very free in giving his opinions," but "this was his character." It did not negate his military competence.[13]

Sherman began worrying about press reaction immediately after the battle, even before any news accounts had appeared. He came on board Admiral D. D. Porter's ship after the fighting's completion looking "as if he had been grappling with the mud and got the worst of it." He expressed his concern over the newspaper reports of the battle. He told the Admiral, a man he admired and trusted, that he had lost 1700 men and "these infernal reporters ... [would] publish all over the country their ridiculous stories about Sherman being whipped etc." He also had a slight though unknown illness, he was angry over being replaced by McClernand, and he was furious about Army rumors that he was under arrest "for disobeying orders in attacking Vixburg [sic] with so small a command."[14] Sherman was again frustrated, and once more he became depressed. The publication of the damning press reports only made matters worse. The world knew of his failure, and his hoped-for success might again be proving to be as elusive as it had always been in the past.

Again he lashed out, and once more newspapers bore the brunt of his criticism. He blamed reporters for his failure; so long as the government allowed Union armies to be "surrounded by such spies" as the press, no success was possible. He argued that the press was unsuccessfully trying to turn his soldiers against him. How he wished he had been killed earlier in the war, so he would not have to face such problems again.[15]

Ellen Sherman agreed with her husband's evaluation of the Vicksburg press accounts, but she joined John Sherman in counseling moderation. She wrote: "if Satan had let all his imps loose upon a special mission of lying we could not have more false information" in the newspapers. Still, she believed he should stop trying to fight reporters; he "might as well attempt to control the whirlwind as the newspaper mania."[16]

Sherman was too angry and disappointed over the press criticism, the failure of the Vicksburg attack, and his replacement by McClernand to be conciliatory. He decided to use his still wide power to try once and for all to silence the press and to place reporters completely under his control. He decided to court-martial a correspondent as a spy. He threatened to "banish" himself to some foreign country if Lincoln interfered with the trial's sentence.[17]

The accused was Thomas W. Knox, although it was obvious from the beginning that Franc B. Wilkie or any other reporter might just as easily have been chosen. The principle not the person was the issue. It was not a matter of trying one reporter; Sherman was attempting to suppress the entire corps of correspondents in the person of Knox. This was a court-martial of the northern press much more than it was merely a court-martial of a well-known correspondent of the powerful *New York Herald*.

Knox had accompanied the Chickasaw Bayou expedition despite the publication of Sherman's order excluding all reporters. He had also been with the Sherman-McClernand expedition to Arkansas Post. He had become friendly with Frank Blair, a scion of the powerful Missouri Blairs, and had, along with Wilkie and Richard T. Colburn of the *New York World*, heard the politician-turned-general criticize his commanding officer. Later rumors credited Knox's critical article, at least in part, to Blair's indiscreet talk.[18] Knox potentially had a powerful sponsor, but it is unknown whether Sherman realized this when he decided to begin court-martial proceedings.

When Sherman made his decision, Knox quickly learned of it. Rumors of the general's intentions, or at least his anger, reached Knox, and, on 1 February 1863 he tried to defuse the matter with an explanatory letter to Sherman. He justified his presence on the Chickasaw Bayou expedition by his ignorance of the exclusion order until after the flotilla had already reached the battle zone. Believing his detention had been ordered, he had gone to the battle field only twice. His account of the battle was "the correct history of the affair," he insisted, even though it was based on "narrow channels of information." Since that time he had seen reports and battle plans, and he now realized he had previously "labored under repeated errors, and made in consequence several mis-statements." He was sorry for the article and was now "fully convinced of your [Sherman's] prompt, efficient and judicious management of the troops under your control from its [the battle's] commencement to its close." In another letter that same day, Knox even offered to correct the original article.[19] He was either sincere in his efforts to present the truth, or else Sherman's court-martial threat had frightened him. The second possibility seems the more probable.

Sherman was not impressed with the reporter's offers of retribution and ordered him arrested upon his appearance in the area. When Knox was brought before the general, he forgot his earlier contrition and displayed an unflinching cockiness. Sherman confronted him with the offending article and he replied: "Of course, General Sherman, I had no feeling against you personally, but you are regarded the enemy of our set, and we must in self-defense write you down." In any case, General Frank Blair was "authority for most of . . . [the] general and specific assertions."[20]

Knox's reply further convinced Sherman of the correctness of his court-martial decision. But first, he wanted to make sure that Knox's accusation against Blair was not true. While Knox was in the Provost Marshal's hands, Sherman wrote Blair, outlining Knox's accusation, and asking for an explanation. Blair hotly denied any wrongdoing. He had not meant anything he may have said in front of Knox to be construed as critical of anyone. Sherman quickly accepted Blair's word and wondered how "a white man [sic] could be so false as this fellow Knox . . . a spy and infamous dog."[21] Obviously, Sherman did not want to battle the powerful Blairs at the same time he was court-martialing Knox. He never pursued the suspicious circumstances any further. He wanted to suppress reporters, not fellow generals.

In another series of letters, Sherman explained his motives for trying Knox as a spy. He assured Admiral Porter that he had no plan to shoot Knox. He simply wanted "to establish the principle that such people cannot attend our armies, in violation of orders, and defy us, publishing their garbled statements and defaming officers who are doing their best." He wrote his brother-in-law that his purpose was "to establish the fact that all civilians whatsoever who follow an army are amenable to Military Law." He told his brother that at issue was the Army's ability to protect itself from internal spies.[22] Sherman was hoping to establish a legal precedent. What happened to Knox was immaterial compared to his desire to gain a legal instrument for keeping reporters away from all future military operations. In Sherman's mind, spying was obviously not the reporters' only sin; their attacks on Army officers were equally valid reasons for their damnation.

The court-martial convened in Sherman's encampment at Young's Point, Louisiana on 5 February 1863.[23] Its president was Volunteer Brigadier General John M. Thayer, and it consisted of six other officers ranging from Colonel to Major. Captain C. Van Rensselaer was the Judge Advocate (the prosecutor). Three charges were leveled against Knox: "Giving intelligence to the enemy, directly or indirectly"; "Being a spy"; and "Disobedience of orders."

The first charge contained two specifications. By accompanying the Chickasaw Bayou expedition and publishing an article which included names of commanders and the strength of one division, Knox was guilty of violating General Orders No. 67 which forbade the printing of any news "without the authority and sanction of the General in command." Knox's article, it was alleged, indirectly gave the enemy an idea of the force's strength and violated the Fifty-Seventh Article of War which General Orders No. 67 had applied to such activity.

The second charge's two specifications accused Knox of boarding the steamer *Continental* despite the well publicized promulgation of Sherman's General Orders No. 8. Knox was also accused of publishing "sundry and various false allegations and accusations against the Officers of the Army of the United States, to the great detriment of the interest of the National Government and comfort of our enemies." A long section from the article in question was cited verbatim.

The two specifications of the third charge claimed that Knox had "knowingly and willfully" disobeyed not only Sherman's exclusion order, but also War Department General Orders No. 67.

After preliminary organizational business, Knox was brought before the tribunal on 7 February. He requested Lieutenant Colonel W. B. Woods as his defense counsel and accepted, without objection, the court-martial board. The charges and specifications were then read to him. He pleaded "not guilty" to the first specification of the third charge (that he "knowingly and willfully" violated Sherman's exclusion order), but refused to plead to anything else. Through his counsel, he pointed out technical defects in the charges and specifications, alleging in sum that they were too general to be legally valid. He cited various sections of military law, but the court sustained only one objection: the one to the second specification of the second charge (that he published false statements against Army officers and thus aided the enemy). Knox then pleaded not guilty to the remaining charges and specifications. He had successfully gained a minor victory in whittling the charges down.

The prosecution opened its case on 10 February by calling Sherman to the stand. He was the prosecution's only witness, actually its entire case. Van Rensselaer tried to delay the proceedings to await the arrival of newspapers allegedly in Admiral

Porter's possession, but the defense objected and was sustained.

Sherman was on the stand for two days, but he presented little that was not already contained in the charges and specifications. His testimony was interrupted innumerable times by defense objections to prosecution questions or Sherman's answers. Practically each time this happened, the court cleared the room for private deliberation. Consequently, the trial's progress was slow.

The prosecution contended, as presented in Sherman's answers, that the commanding general's personal observation and his spies proved that information printed about the Union Army in northern newspapers regularly appeared in the southern press. The defense countered that this proved nothing. The existence of northern press material in southern newspapers, even if proven, was not relevant in this case. The prosecution had to prove that Knox's article had actually been copied and that the enemy had actually seen it. Suppositions about articles in general, even when corroborated, were irrelevant.

When it came time for the defense counsel to cross-examine Sherman, he asked only one question: the name of the commander of the Thirteenth Army Corps during the Chickasaw Bayou attack. Sherman answered: Grant. The prosecution quickly redirected, asking if Grant had been present with that portion of the thirteenth corps which had assaulted the Vicksburg heights. Sherman said no and was excused. The prosecution made one more futile attempt to delay the trial to await the newspapers

The Press on Trial 147

from Porter, then introduced General Orders No. 67, and rested its case.

The defense now presented its side. Knox's counsel, Lieutenant Colonel W. B. Woods, called upon the reporter's former school teacher Colonel Isaac Shepherd of the Third Missouri Infantry Regiment, Brigadier Generals Francis P. (Frank) Blair and Frederick Steele, and William E. Webb of the *St. Louis Missouri Republican* as character witnesses. All spoke in glowing terms of Knox's loyalty and reliability. The defense also argued that General Orders No. 67 had been modified and reporters in McClellan's army given permission to give details of a battle after the fighting was over. Knox's article had been written four days after the end of the Chickasaw Bayou fighting when Sherman's army had already been twenty-five miles away. Finally, the defense argued, Knox had had a right to accompany the expedition despite Sherman's order, because he had possessed a pass from Grant, the commander of the Thirteenth Army Corps, to which Sherman's expeditionary force belonged.

These were all telling arguments, and the prosecution moved to undercut them by recalling Sherman. The commanding general said he had never seen Knox's pass from Grant, and McClellan's modification of General Orders No. 67 had never been "officially communicated" to him. He was unaware of any other modifications.

Except for his testimony and sending pertinent material about the trial to Grant so he might "see the truth amid the cloud of falsehood and defamation," Sherman could not legally influence the court proceedings any further. But they were always on his mind. "Shall the orders of the War Department be respected? Or shall the press go on sweeping everything before it. . . . If the press can govern this country, let them fight the battles." Friends and relatives tried to calm him, but his anger continued unabated. He inferred from the court's periodic rulings that, in order to bring Knox within the jurisdiction of the Fifty-Seventh Article of War as promulgated in General Orders No. 67, the prosecution would have to prove that the enemy had actually read the offending article. He realized this was impossible and insisted that the common knowledge of the southern newspaper practice of publishing northern articles was enough to convict Knox. He lamented that the court was "more or less afraid of the press," so chances for a favorable decision were slim.[24]

He remained depressed and continued to pour out his heart to relatives and friends. He blamed newspapers for the paralysis of the Army of the Potomac and for all the other failures of the war. The successful western battles, Arkansas Post and Forts Henry and Donelson, he said, had been possible only because reporters had been kept away. Newspapers served no useful purpose; soldiers' letters home kept the North sufficiently informed on the war's progress. His purpose in this trial as in all his anti-press activities was to try to eliminate a source of intelligence, leakage, and interofficer discord. His loyalty to the Union remained strong, but he would resign before he would kow-tow to reporters. He had learned an important lesson in this war; he had to look more closely to his own interests and "less to the demands of the public, that ... [was] so ready to believe all that ... [was] infamous" of him. He told some old friends from California and St. Louis that he hoped they would remember him in case any suitable business venture materialized.[25] Once more, Sherman's frustration and depression made him think of quitting the Army.

In the meantime, the court-martial was drawing to a close. On the morning of 14 February the defense and the prosecution presented their final arguments.[26] Knox himself wrote the defense statement, but defense counsel Wood read it to the court.

Knox's statement began by reminding the court of its duty to make a decision only on evidence presented during the trial and to find him guilty only when such evidence proved his guilt "beyond reasonable doubt." Otherwise, the court had to find him innocent. The prosecution case, Knox said, had not proven his guilt. He had written the article in question, but McClellan's modification of General Orders No. 67 (which, he said, applied to the entire Army) permitted the publication of unit's and commander's names after the completion of a battle. He had written his report four days after the battle when the Union Army was already twenty-five miles away from Vicksburg.

Knox also insisted that the prosecution had not proven several major contentions: that he had written his battle account to inform the enemy; that the article's content was dangerous; and that the enemy had seen it. The prosecution had never even proven that any *New York Herald* had ever reached enemy hands. "The fact that a thing might possibly happen does not prove or tend to prove that it has happened."

Sherman's General Orders No. 8 had not applied to him, Knox continued, even if the prosecution had proven he had been aware of it. The order prevented only those in the service of the United States or the transports from writing anything for publication. Others were excluded from being on board. Since he had a pass from Grant, who knew he was a reporter, this permission was his sufficient authority for writing the article.

The defense witnesses had shown him, Knox concluded, to be a man of character and loyalty. He felt mortified at having his patriotism questioned, but he stood ready to make necessary corrections in an admittedly error-laden article. He left the verdict confidently in the hands of the court, "men without fear and without reproach." He felt sure "that humble as is his station and high as is the character and position of his accuser, his every right will be protected and justice will be done him."

After a brief recess, the Judge Advocate, Captain C. Van Rensselaer, presented the prosecution side. In a highly organized presentation, he listed the letter, Knox's admission he wrote it, and the fact that Sherman had not authorized it as evidence against Knox. The reporter's presence on a military transport, without Sherman's permission and in violation of the officially promulgated General Orders No. 67 and No. 8, was also part of the evidence. Finally, Sherman, "who from custom and necessity had had every means of knowing," was sure that material from the northern press "very often" appeared in southern newspapers.

The key point, Van Rensselaer said, was that General Orders No. 67 had to be interpreted. The section which read "shall reach the enemy" really meant "may or might reach the enemy." "There is a general presumption in capital cases that a person intends whatever is the natural and probable consequence of his actions." A newspaper man who writes an article containing information useful to the enemy in a paper known to be read by the enemy is guilty of leaking secrets. His intent, unless he can prove otherwise, is to aid the enemy.

Knox's defense, the Judge Advocate argued, was inadequate. Protestations of his character were irrevelant. McClellan's modification of General Orders No. 67, the so-called Notice to a Correspondent, had no validity in any western army. Sherman's General Orders No. 8 superceded everything that had come before it. Possession of a pass from Grant was equally specious; a pass kept in a pocket was useless and, besides, Knox's pass had been superceded by competent military authority (i.e. Sherman) sometime after its issuance.

Finally, the prosecution argued, public safety required the strict enforcement of all pertinent rules and regulations

> The discipline of military powers and authority is claimed to have been violated. It must be sustained. The safety of our Army is claimed to have been endangered: it should be secured.
>
> The interests of our cause are claimed to have been im-

perilled [sic]: they should be placed where the hand of danger cannot reach.

With closing arguments completed, the court went into closed session. Four days later it found Knox not guilty of the first and second charges; he was not guilty of violating the Fifty-Seventh Article of War. He was guilty of the third charge, but, as for the specification that he violated Sherman's order by accompanying the expedition, the court ruled "the facts proven as stated, but attaches no criminality thereto." Knox was ordered outside Army lines under threat of arrest.[27]

Sherman became livid and wrote to Grant's Adjutant demanding that he send the verdict through channels to the General-in-chief for review. Two specific aspects of the decision particularly angered him. He argued that the court's statement, seeing no criminality in Knox's presence with the expedition despite Sherman's order, inferred "that a commanding officer has no right to prohibit citizens from accompanying a military expedition, or if he does, such citizens incur no criminality by disregarding such command." Secondly, he protested the court's decision that Knox's article had provided the Confederates with no information. It was impossible to track a particular article down behind enemy lines, but it was legally sufficient to note that their press was full of clippings from northern newspapers. "I believe," he concluded, "this cause [freedom of the press] has lost us millions of money, thousands of lives, and will continue to defeat us to the end of time, unless some remedy be devised."[28]

Sherman vented his emotions further in letters to his family. He threatened to quit the Army in disgust over the court-martial's decision. He worried his father-in-law/foster-father, Thomas Ewing, so much that Ewing wrote his son, a member of Sherman's staff, urging him to impress on Sherman that his resignation "would be a terrible mortification to his family and a triumph to his enemies." Hugh Ewing wrote back that Sherman seemed content and displayed no thoughts of resignation.[29] As always, Sherman's letters home were a way of letting off steam.

Toward the end of February, Sherman's anger seemed to be abating because he promised his wife he would no longer try to exclude the "buzzards of the press" from his camp. But this proved illusory. The reception of a series of letters whose anti-press tone rivaled his own stimulated him again. General Edward Ord wrote him that a dying Democratic Party, in its attempt to preserve itself, had purchased a number of Ohio and Indiana newspapers. Any general who opposed the Democrats would be flattened. Ellen Sherman suspected Ord of secessionist leanings and urged her husband to ignore him, but then she threw off her own moderation and encouraged him to sue the *St. Louis Missouri Democrat* and the *Cincinnati Gazette*. Sherman again ignored such advice, but this did not prevent him from making some foolish statements of his own. He predicted Jefferson Davis planned to win the war by spending "a few thousand of dollars" to take over the northern press. Newspapers had defeated him and they would destroy the nation, he said. "Napoleon himself would have been defeated with a free press."[30]

While Sherman was raving against the decision (losing sight of the fact that Knox, after all, had been banished), newspapers maintained a discreet silence. Even the *New York Herald* did not support its own reporter. Only three papers commented on the case in any depth, and one, the *Washington Chronicle*, even took Sherman's side. (John Sherman provided it with pertinent correspondence.) The *New York Tribune* said this case indicated that Sherman seemed determined to prove that the allegations of his insanity were true. But it said nothing further. The *St. Louis Missouri Republican*'s reporter William E. Webb, one of Knox's character witnesses, described the court-martial as a test case to see "whether military power" could be used "for the gratification of private malice" and whether "just criticism [would] be suppressed." Knox had been the victim of an "arbitrary arrest,"[31] but the court's decision had vindicated him and the press.

The Missouri newspaper soon changed its position. Despite the fact that it was still sniping at Sherman as late as 25 February, it did a complete turnabout on 15 March. With the fervor of a convert, probably brought to the fount of truth by Sherman's St. Louis friends, the *Missouri Republican* ran a series of editorials echoing Sherman's position on the Knox case. The newspaper warned its readers to remember that reporters often endangered their lives to publish "a startling item of intelligence in advance of a rival contemporary." Such an attitude was an obvious threat to successful military operations. At Vicksburg, reporters had violated General Orders No. 67 by accompanying the expedition and then publishing information of value to the enemy. It made no sense to criticize Sherman because, after learning the facts, even a correspondent "who was one of the harshest critics" (obviously Knox) had admitted his error. As in Kentucky, the truth about Vicksburg would "bring confusion to his [Sherman's] detractors and award him the approval of all calm and unbiased minds." Had he captured Vicksburg, that which was "now berated as insanity would have been extolled as patriotism."[32]

Northern newspapers, then, virtually ignored the obviously ominous court-martial of a reporter. Newspapers may have considered this incident an aberration and decided to ignore it; but, considering Sherman's reputation and the government efforts at censorship, this Knox case could well have been a precedent for more effective future press restrictions. T. A. Post of the *New York Tribune* warned his editor of just this possibility. He said that Sherman viewed the Knox trial as a "precedent," hoping to gag the press by prosecuting any reporter who criticized any military man. He hoped the *Tribune* would, at least, treat Knox fairly.[33] The *Tribune*, like most papers, apparently feared repercussions and remained silent.

Despite Sherman's anger over the court-martial's leniency, he had actually won a major victory. Knox had been banished, and newspapers offered no effective protest. Sherman had accomplished at least part of his aim. In the future, newspapers would treat him carefully and, thereby, allow him more leeway to thwart them. He now had the advantage, although, in his anger, he did not realize it. At least, though, he was rid of Knox. Or so it seemed.

In Washington, several reporters decided to try to help their banished colleague. Though their newspapers had not defended Knox in print, they drew up a memorial contending that Knox's loyalty and the obsolescence of the Article of War in question were grounds for reversing the banishment sentence. Two newspaper men and the congressional delegate from Knox's prewar residence, Colorado, presented the memorial to Abraham Lincoln. The two reporters were Albert D. Richardson of the *New York Tribune*, Knox's old colleague, and James M. Mitchell of the *New York Times*. Lincoln received the delegation warmly and traded stories with Richardson, a prewar acquaintance. He said he was willing to "serve" any loyal journalist at any time, but, for the present, the nation's generals were even more important than the president. He wanted "to do nothing whatsoever which ... [could] possibly embarass [sic] any of them." But he would write a letter on Knox's behalf. Richardson, who had engaged the president in an animated discussion of the case, was forced to give in. "There was too much irresistible good sense in this to permit any further discussion." Reporter Mitchell agreed. Lincoln had effectively but graciously sidetracked the delegation.[34]

Lincoln composed the letter in front of the delegation on a document littered table; it was a masterpiece of evasion. Addressed to "whom it may concern," it said that, since General Thayer, the President of the Court-Martial board, and "many other respectable persons" including General McClernand were "of the opinion that Mr. Knox's offense was technical rather than wilfull [sic] wrong," Knox could proceed to Grant's camp. It was Grant, however, who would have to decide whether Knox could remain.[35] Lincoln thus mollified the reporters without giving the military cause for anger.

Lincoln's letter was quickly sent to Knox and, armed with it, he arrived at Grant's camp at the beginning of April. Grant read the letter and, in reply, wrote a stinging indictment of the reporter. He would not allow him to stay unless Sherman agreed. Knox immediately wrote to Sherman and enclosed Lincoln's letter. He told Sherman that Grant had no objection to his return if Sherman agreed. "Without referring in detail to past occurrences," Knox expressed his "regret at the want of harmony between portions of the Army and the Press" and hoped for better relations in the future. Sherman's "favor in the matter . . . [would] be duly appreciated" by himself and the paper he represented.[36]

Sherman exploded. He regretted that Thayer and McClernand regarded Knox's actions "as mere technical offenses" and reminded Knox of his comments about the necessity for reporters to attack all those who stood in the way of the "fraternity" and of his assertion that the press had the right to publish false news. He then totally rejected Knox's appeal:

> Come with sword or musket in your hand, prepared to share with us our fate, in sunshine and storm, in prosperity and adversity, in plenty and scarcity and I will welcome you as brother and associate. But come as you now do expecting me to ally the honor and reputation of my country and my fellow soldiers with you, as the representative of the press, which you yourself say makes so slight a difference between truth and falsehood, and my answer is, Never.[37]

Knox understood the hopelessness of his cause and soon moved to the Eastern theater of the war where he reported other military engagements including the battle of Gettysburg. In later life, he travelled widely, wrote over forty books about his experiences, and was awarded the Siamese Order of the White Elephant for one of these travelogues. In one book he urged that in future wars reporters be protected from wrathful generals by making them part of the military establishment. In retrospect, he felt his "little quarrel with General Sherman . . . [had] proved 'a blessing in disguise.' " Had Sherman not banished him, he would certainly have accompanied reporters Richardson, Browne, and Colburn in their attempt to sneak past the Vicksburg batteries. Their boat was blown out of the water, they were all captured, and spent twenty months in a Confederate prison.[38]

Thus, Sherman was successful in keeping Knox out and establishing the precedent, with Lincoln's tacit acknowledgement, that a journalist could only accompany a military unit if he was acceptable to the field commander (later called accredidation). Despite this precedent-setting victory, Sherman was still angry and continued to lash out at reporters and those who in any way had disagreed with his court-martial stand. He blamed Thayer's support for Knox as a repayment for an earlier newspaper eulogy. As for McClernand, "he would sign the death warrant of his son for a newspaper puff." "Knox is simply nobody," he wrote, "but he represents the Press, and as such expects to rule the country." Lincoln had to make a choice: rule the *New York Herald* or be ruled by it. Either newspapers were controlled, or constitutional government was finished. He was "no enemy to freedom of thought, freedom of the 'press' and speech," he said unconvincingly, "but in all controversies there . . . [was] a time [when] discussion . . . [had to] cease and action begin." "All I propose to say is that Mr. Lincoln and the press may, in the exercise of their glorious prerogative, tear our country and armies to tatters; but they shall not insult me with impunity in my own camp."[39]

Sherman was in an ugly mood. When he learned about the three reporters being blown out of the Mississippi waters near Vicksburg, he supposedly said: "Good! Now we'll have news from hell before breakfast." The government refusal to face the reality of the military-press situation as he saw it was exasperating. His letters home were so harsh that his wife warned him not to commit any "act of violence" and be "charged with the life of a poor wretch unfit for earth."[40] Again he was simply venting his frustrations, but these letters showed the intensity of his continued hatred for reporters and his unwillingness to recognize that they might have a role to play in the war effort.

It must be remembered, too, that "the camp around Vicksburg could not have been improved upon as a breeding place for irascibility." Grant, Sherman, and their Union forces were bogged down trying to build canals to divert the Mississippi River and cause it to flow in a new channel distant from Vicksburg's imposing heights. The work was hard, dirty, and monotonous with little diversion to break the routine. When one such diversion developed for Sherman, it only intensified his press hatred. He was meeting with Confederate officers to discuss an exchange of prisoners, and Union troops were using the opportunity to secretly set up batteries near Vicksburg. To Sherman's disgust, the Memphis press divulged the secret. At one of the parlays, a Confederate coyly asked Sherman not to fire the supposedly secret batteries that evening, because he was going to a party and did not want to be disturbed. Grant suppressed the culprits, the *Memphis Bulletin* and *Argus*, but this action did not satisfy Sherman. He continued to insist that total exclusion of noncombatants from Army camps was the only way to prevent the leakage of such information in the future.[41]

The court-martial of Reporter Thomas W. Knox is the most famous military trial of a newspaper man in American history. It took place because William T. Sherman's animosity toward reporters had evolved into a belief that such action was essential to the war effort. Knox symbolized the entire northern press corps. Sherman was not concerned with Knox as much as he was determined to establish a legal precedent for excluding all newspaper reporters from battle areas. He believed that any war news, no matter how trivial, aided the enemy; therefore none should appear in the newspapers. At least, an effective system of censorship was essential to prevent the publication of information dangerous to Union arms. Since his definition of information valuable to the enemy was so broad and included any criticism of military men, practically nothing about the war could be printed. Sherman hoped in this trial to gain the power to control the press totally. His position was in direct conflict with the Bill of Rights guarantee of freedom of the press. He was arguing that the military had the right and duty to prevent the publication of all war news. Total censorship, as defined by the military, had to be instituted in order to wage war effectively. A democracy could only fight a war by eliminating (not merely regulating) part of its creed, freedom of the press. The Constitution was not only to be "put on the shelf" for the war's duration, it was to be fundamentally altered. Paradoxically, Sherman's anti-press views were a threat to the document, the Constitution, he so revered and in whose defense he fought. What made the situation even more dangerous was his inability to recognize this fact.

The newspapers' reaction to the Knox trial, more correctly their lack of reaction, indicates that Sherman had successfully frightened them. Newspapers, which had again called Sherman insane for his part in the Chickasaw Bayou debacle, were now silent at the sacrifice of one of their number and the threat to their collective safety. Sherman was unhappy over the court-martial decision because he had not been able to establish the all-encompassing precedent he had sought. Judging by the newspaper silence, however, he had been more successful than he realized. He had established the precedent of military accreditation of newsmen and had so frightened reporters that they made little protest. The Knox court-martial was a turning point in the relations between Sherman and newsmen. Up to this point he had feared reporters; now they feared him. He had not gained a total victory, but what happened was significant nonetheless. Sherman had pushed his anti-press views to their logical conclusion—use of military power to exclude reporters completely and establish total censorship. While he failed to achieve this aim in the court-martial, he later succeeded during his famous marches. His failure to gain the legal precedent he felt he needed proved no barrier to the successful implementation of his anti-newspaper views in the future.

No one had ever court-martialed a reporter before and no one would do it in the future, not even during the often hysterical days of World War I nor during the bitter days of the Vietnam conflict. No government official ever dared do what Sherman did; yet, Sherman's court-martial of a reporter remains a symbol of the danger war always causes for the Bill of Rights. The most ominous fact is that, throughout the trial and the commentary that followed, the Constitution was never mentioned by Sherman or the press. Personal not constitutional considerations were the main issue, even though the First Amendment was on trial with Knox.

NOTES

1. For accounts of Sherman's role in this battle, see B. H. Liddell Hart, *Sherman: Soldier, Realist, American* (New York, 1958), pp. 160–165, and James M. Merrill, *William Tecumseh Sherman* (New York, 1971), pp. 213–215. Lloyd Lewis, *Sherman: Fighting Prophet* (New York, 1932), pp. 255-259 emphasizes that Grant pushed the attack too quickly in order to launch it before the arrival of political general John McClernand. In an article, Herman Hattaway criticizes Sherman, arguing that Stephen D. Lee's success here "added a great deal to the myth of superiority of Confederate command." Hattaway, "Confederate Myth Making: Top Command and the Chickasaw Bayou Campaign," *Journal of Mississippi History* 32 (November 1970): 311–326.

2. William T. Sherman to "My Dear Children," 8 December 1862, William T. Sherman Papers, Ohio Historical Society; General Orders No. 8, Hq., Right Wing, 13th Army Corps, William T. Sherman Papers, Library of Congress. Hereafter cited as: WTS Papers, LC.

3. Charles D. Firebaugh, "General William T. Sherman's Attitude Toward the Newspaper Press, 1861–1865," master's thesis, Ohio State University, 1958, pp. 81–82; *New York Tribune*, 1, 12 January 1863.

4. Sylvanus Cadwallader, *Three Years With Grant*, ed. Benjamin P. Thomas (New York, 1956), p. 45; J. Cutler

Andrews, *The North Reports the Civil War* (Pittsburgh, 1953), pp. 376–377.

5. William H. Seward, "Diary or Notes on the War," *The Works of William H. Seward*, ed. George E. Baker (Boston, 1884), 6: 88; *New York Herald*, 12 January 1863.

6. *Louisville Journal*, 13 January 1863; *Chicago Tribune*, 13, 14, 15 January 1863.

7. *Cincinnati Gazette*, 15 January 1863.

8. *Louisville Journal*, 16 January 1863; *New York Times*, 19 January 1863; *Cincinnati Gazette*, 31 January 1863.

9. Franc B. Wilkie, *Pen and Powder* (Boston, 1888), p. 237; *New York Times*, 18, 19 January 1863.

10. Ibid.

11. Wilkie, pp. 237, 245–247, 365–367.

12. *New York Herald*, 18 January 1863.

13. *Cincinnati Commercial*, 24 January, 2 February 1863. The *Commercial* also printed a sketch of Sherman's life and left out any mention of the 1861 insanity controversy.

14. WTS to John Sherman, 6 January 1863, WTS Papers, LC; David D. Porter, *Incidents and Anecdotes of the Civil War* (New York, 1885), p. 129; L. N. Dayton to Ellen Sherman, 14 January 1863; WTS Papers, LC; Carlos W. Colby, "Bullets, Hardtack and Mud: A Soldier's View of the Vicksburg Campaign," ed. John S. Painter, *Journal of the West* 4 (April 1865): 135; Allan Nevins, in his monumental work on the Civil War, states that McClernand's arrival found "the defeated Sherman glad to subside into a position of a corps commander." He obviously bases this belief on a statement Sherman made in an official letter. The mass of Sherman's correspondence, however, shows he was angry, not happy, at McClernand's arrival. Allan Nevins, *War for the Union* (New York, 1960), 2: 384.

15. WTS to JS, 17, 25, 31 January 1863, WTS Papers, LC; WTS to Ellen Sherman, 24, 28 January 1863, Sherman Family Papers, University of Notre Dame Archives. Hereafter cited as: S. F. P., UNDA.

16. ES to WTS, 19 January 1863, ibid.

17. WTS to ES, 28 January 1863, ibid.

18. William E. Smith, *The Francis Preston Blair Family in Politics* (New York, 1933), 2: 152. Smith argues that Knox's account was not based on Blair's gossiping.

19. Thomas W. Knox to WTS, 1 February 1863, *War of the Rebellion ... Official Records of the Union and Confederate Armies* (Washington, 1880-1901), Ser I, 17, pt. 2: 580–581. Hereafter cited as: *O. R.* Knox to WTS, 1 February 1863, WTS Papers, LC; Knox, *Campfire and Cottonfield* (New York, 1865), p. 254.

20. WTS to Murat Halstead, 8 April 1863, *O. R.* Ser. I, 17, pt. 2: 896.

21. WTS to F. P. Blair, 1 February 1863, Blair to WTS, 1 February 1863, WTS to Blair, 2, 3 February 1863, *O. R.* Ser. I, 17, pt. 2: 581-590.

22. D. D. Porter to WTS, WTS to Porter, 3 February 1863, WTS Papers, LC; WTS to Porter, 4 February 1863, *O. R.* Ser. I, 17, pt. 2: 889; WTS to Hugh Ewing, 4 February 1863, William T. Sherman Papers, Ohio Historical Society; WTS to JS, 4 February 1863, WTS Papers, LC.

23. The following account of this court-martial is based on the original court-martial records: Court-Martial of Thomas W. Knox, Records of the Judge Advocate General (Army), Record Group 153, LL 154, National Archives and Records Service, Washington.

24. WTS to John Rawlins, 4 February 1863, *O. R.* Ser. I, 17, pt. 1: 763; WTS to JS, 7 February 1863, WTS Papers, LC; ES to WTS, 8, 11 February 1863, S. F. P., UNDA; Officers of the Second and Third Brigade of the 15th

Army Corps to U. S. Grant, 10 February 1863, JS to WTS, 10 February 1863, E. Ord to WTS, 13 February 1863, WTS to JS, 12 February 1863, WTS Papers, LC.

25. WTS to James H. Lucas, et. al., 9 February 1863, Thomas Ewing Papers, Library of Congress. Hereafter cited as: TE Papers, LC.

26. See note 23.

27. Ibid: charges, specifications and decision were also published in General Orders No. 13, Hq., Dept. of the Tennessee, 19 February 1863, *O. R.*, Ser. I, 17, pt. 2: 889–892.

28. WTS to John Rawlins, 23 February 1863, ibid., pp. 892-893.

29. Thomas Ewing to Hugh Ewing, copy, 25 February 1863, Hugh Ewing to Thomas Ewing, 15 March 1863, TE Papers, LC.

30. WTS to ES, 22, 26 February 1863, S. F. P., UNDA; E. Ord to WTS, 6 March 1863, quoted in Braxton Bragg et. al., "Some More War Letters," ed. S. M. H. Byers, *North American Review* 144 (April 1887), 379; ES to WTS, 7, 9, 13, 26 March 1863, S. F. P., UNDA; WTS to JS, 14 March 1863, WTS Papers, LC.

31. *Washington Chronicle*, 16 February 1863; *New York Tribune*, 18 February 1863. A Boston newspaper similarly said that Sherman's actions in this case seemed "to corroborate" the insanity. *Boston Journal*, 3 March 1863, quoted in Thomas H. Guback, "Control and Censorship of the Northern Press During the Civil War," bachelors thesis, Rutgers University, 1958, p. 116; *St. Louis Missouri Republican*, 14, 20 February 1863.

32. Ibid., 25 February, 15, 16 March 1863.

33. T. A. Post to Sydney Howard Gay, 6 February 1863, Sydney Howard Gay Papers, Butler Library, Columbia University.

34. Albert D. Richardson, *Secret Service: The Field, the*

Dungeon and the Escape (Hartford, 1865), pp. 318-320; J. M. Winchell, "Three Interviews with President Lincoln," *The Galaxy* 16 (July 1873): 33–34.

35. Lincoln to whom it may concern, 20 March 1863, *O. R.*, Ser. I, 17, pt. 2: 894.

36. Grant to Knox, 6 April 1863, Knox to WTS, 6 April 1863, ibid., pp. 894-895.

37. WTS to Knox, 7 April 1863, ibid., pp. 894-895.

38. Knox, *Campfire and Cottonfield*, p. 490; T. L. Christie, "The General and the News 'Spy' " *Saturday Review* 50 (8 July 1967): 65.

39. Edwin Emery, *The Press and America*, 3rd ed. (Englewood Cliffs, N. J., 1972), p. 243; WTS to JS, copy, 7 April 1863, S. F. P., UNDA; WTS to Grant, 9 April 1863, WTS to Murat Halstead, 8 April 1863, *O. R.*, Ser. I, 17, pt. 2: 895–897.

40. Knox, p. 260; Junius H. Browne, *Four Years in Secessia* (Hartford, 1865), p. 238; ES to WTS, 9 April 1863, S. F. P., UNDA.

41. Bernard A. Weisberger, *Reporters for the Union* (Boston, 1953), p. 277; WTS to JS, 10 April 1863, WTS Papers, LC; *Cincinnati Commercial*, 14, 16 April 1863; *Cincinnati Gazette*, 15, 16 April 1863; *Washington Star*, 16 April 1863; WTS to ES, 10 April 1863, S. F. P., UNDA; WTS to TE, 13 April 1863, TE Papers, LC.

6
The March Minus Reporters

As SPRING 1863 turned into summer, the Vicksburg siege continued. The increasingly hot, sticky weather made the dull backbreaking work of canal and trench digging correspondingly more exhausting. Progress was slow; Vicksburg seemed more impregnable each day as the Mississippi River refused to be diverted to a new channel by Federal shovels. Spirits were low, and confusion was rampant. Union forces seemed incapable of capturing the Gibraltar on the Mississippi.

Newspapers mirrored this uncertainty. Throughout that spring, contradictory rumors filled newspapers columns. As early as 22 April 1863, the *New York Herald* reported the Confederate evacuation of Vicksburg. On 25 May it headlined: "Vicksburg is Ours." On the twenty-seventh, it admitted its mistake, but two days later again reported rumors of Vicksburg's capture, only to have to retract the following week.[1]

This press confusion continued into the summer

months. Reporters did not understand Grant's brilliant maneuver resulting in the 4 July surrender of Vicksburg. Even the exact date of that besieged city's fall was at first unclear. The first news of Vicksburg's capture reached the North by the most roundabout route. The *Louisville Journal*'s experience was typical. On 4 July 1863 the *Journal* reported under a 2 July Baltimore heading that the *Philadelphia Inquirer* bulletin board had announced the Navy Yard's discovery of Vicksburg's capture. But, even this circuitous announcement was premature. The North did not receive definitive confirmation of the 4 July surrender until 8 July. Newspapers, so often wrong in the past, now used headlines like: "Vicksburg is Ours Without Doubt!" and "The Good News Fully Confirmed."[2]

Newspaper space about Vicksburg was sparse compared to the fanfare accorded Gettysburg, the battle in southeastern Pennsylvania that occurred at the same time. Sherman's name was seldom seen, his subordinate role under Grant and his recent encounters with Knox apparently limiting his appeal to reporters. Because newspapers said so little about him and his army, Sherman made few comments about reporters. When he did, however, it was typically hostile. He wrote Grant to congratulate him on the victory and said that, except for their friendship, he "would be tempted to follow the example of . . . [his] standard enemies of the press in indulging in wanton flattery." Instead, he warned Grant against such plaudits. Grant's success in defeating "a brave but deluded enemy . . . [had been] more eloquent than the most gorgeous oratory of an [Edward] Everett" and spoke for itself without need for flattery.³

Sherman was now part of a major success, a circumstance made doubly sweet by the press ignorance which surrounded it. Unfortunately, he had little time to savor the circumstance. He felt exhausted and suffered either from an injury or an illness. Precisely what the problem was is unknown, but it was sufficiently serious to cause Lincoln to express concern and Ellen Sherman to send a Notre Dame priest. The *Cincinnati Gazette* and the *New York Tribune* reported his death in New Orleans while having his leg amputated, although the *Tribune* later said he was actually in Newport, Rhode Island.⁴

Whatever the problem, and perhaps it was simply camp rumor or wishful thinking on the part of reporters, Sherman's family paid him a two-month visit in late August. He enjoyed their company and took them on tours of the battle sites. In early October, disaster struck. Nine-year-old Willie, Sherman's favorite, became ill with typhoid fever and died on his way home. Sherman blamed himself for exposing his son to typhoid germs; Ellen shared in the guilt feelings. For months, the tragedy stayed with them both, Sherman seeing his dead son whether "Sleeping—walking—everywhere."⁵

Fortunately, the months of post-Vicksburg inactivity ended, and Sherman kept his promise to Halleck that his son's death would not "divert . . . [his] mind from the duty . . . he owe[d] . . . his country."⁶ In October when Grant was made commander of the Western theater, Sherman was promoted to

Grant's former position, as commander of the Army of the Tennessee. His place in the Army hierarchy was secure despite the recent controversies of Chickasaw Bayou and the Knox court-martial.

It did not take him long to brandish his increased power before newspaper reporters. He saw a newspaper column he considered improper and fired off a letter to S. A. Hurlbut, Sixth Army Corps commander in Memphis, to warn newspapers there not to publish "too much nonsense." "No anonymous letters, no praise or censure of officers, no discussion of the policy and measures of the Government without [*sic*] the article is reviewed by the commanding officer at Memphis, and [the] editor [made] responsible for the general tenor of extracts of other papers." Hurlbut issued the grammatically garbled order, but Sherman still fumed. He told a subordinate of his intention to "stop all such trash hereafter from originating in Memphis." Not satisfied with subordinates' admonitions he twice warned editors of the *Memphis Bulletin* personally and with obvious relish:

> Now I am again in authority over you, and you must heed my advice. Freedom of speech and freedom of the Press, precious relics of former history, must not be construed too largely. You must print nothing that prejudices government or excites envy, hatred, and malice in a community. Persons in office or out of office must not be flattered or abused. Don't publish an account of any skirmish, battle or movement of an army unless the name of the writer is given in full and printed. I wish you success, but my first duty is to maintain "order and harmony."

Memphis newspapers had the right to criticize the

government, he continued, if they did it "in the proper spirit and [in a manner] designed to do good." The formula for newspaper success was to tell the truth, aim to do good, and not cause resentment. Business should be encouraged, the past narrated, and, "when well authenticated," the present discussed.[7]

These nebulous statements, doubly ominous because of their imprecise nature, worried the *Bulletin* and its editor immediately asked for a clarification. Sherman was happy to oblige, and his answer showed clearly that he had not developed a cohesive philosophy on a subject which was consuming so much of his time and energy. He frankly admitted that he did not have a clear definition of freedom of the press. He believed in it all right, "in freedom as near absolute as . . . [was] consistent with safety." At the same time, he believed press freedom had to be limited to prevent evil. Both in peacetime as in war, newspapers had responsibilities as well as freedoms. During war, the press, like everything else in society, had to be subordinated to the war effort. The president, "by his army and navy must control all the physique and morals of the nation to restore such peace and quiet as will enable the courts to resume their sway." Until courts were restored, the military had to provide law or else anarchy would ensue. "Nature abhors anarchy." Once the conflict was over, military control should end, and press freedom, like everything else, could then be restored to normal. During war, however, he emphasized that press freedoms had to be tightly controlled.[8]

These statements show Sherman's complete adherence to total war and his belief that, in fighting a war, organization for victory was the only matter of importance. Nothing, not even the Bill of Rights, could be allowed to stand in the way of triumph. Sherman was clearly an adherent of the view that in crisis the Constitution had to be set aside. The survival of authority, what a later generation would call "law and order," was more important to him than the continuation of basic civil rights. He believed that press privileges might particularly be curtailed because he thought newspapers performed no essential function. The people were able to learn enough about the war from soldiers' letters home and from commanders' official reports. Newspapers, therefore, were redundant and their suppression, even their elimination, would cause no hardship to anyone but newsmen.

Sherman's strong statements to the *Memphis Bulletin* were only the most obvious manifestations of a renewed policy of newspaper restriction. He screwed the clamp of censorship down tightly. The *New York Herald* complained that "all news of military operations in that quarter . . . [was] contraband." Reporters feared his wrath and gave him a wide berth. Even Henry Villard, his nighttime companion in the Kentucky telegraph office, avoided him. "In the face of these fulminations [letters to the *Bulletin*], it naturally seemed the part of discretion to keep away," Villard later explained.[9] Consequently, Sherman received little press notice. He took part in the battle of Chattanooga and strengthened Ambrose Burnside at Knoxville, but these activities were not covered in any depth.

He continued to grieve over his son's death, and his wife sent him nearly hysterical letters of grief and guilt on the same subject. Fortunately, he was able to avoid serious depression. He took Christmas leave in December 1863 and visited his family into January, and this helped.[10] The respite allowed him to prepare himself physically and emotionally for the hard months that lay ahead.

Even as he rested during the Christmas break he did not relax his anti-press bias. It was suggested to him that he commission John Sherman's secretary, *Cincinnati Commercial* reporter, Joseph McCullagh, to write a biography. His answer was sharp. The final stages of the war would determine the heroes, and "Newspaper puffs, & self-written biographies . . . [would] then be ridiculous caricatures." Expressing a confidence not often with him, he said he believed that, next to Grant, he was the leading officer on the Mississippi. He needed no court historian.[11]

When he returned to Tennessee, he continued his harsh censorship. In late January and early February 1864 he undertook a raid through Mississippi, cutting a swath of destruction from Vicksburg, through Jackson, to Meridian. He entered Mississippi's capital on 4 February and was in Meridian ten days later. Newspaper reporters were aware of his expedition, but Sherman concealed its precise nature and his exact whereabouts from them. At first, reporters blamed their lack of hard news on the need for military secrecy, but they soon dropped that ploy and began to try to pinpoint Sherman's location. They placed him at such widely scattered points as Marietta, Georgia, Selma, Alabama, and Mobile. The *New York Herald* said he was "getting along swimmingly," his expedition being the "boldest of the war." The tone changed when newspapers realized they had been hoodwinked. The *New York Herald* now called the "bold movement" merely an "extended reconnaissance," and moaned: "The anxiety to know something about General Sherman's whereabouts and safety has become intense." Newspapers admitted Sherman had completely concealed his activities from their reporters.[12]

Sherman had fully accomplished his long desired aim to impose a total embargo on news from his Army, and he reacted to this success with unconcealed delight. His expedition, he wrote, "certainly baffled the sharp ones of the Press and stampeded all Alabama." "Had I tolerated a corps of Newspaper men how could I have made that March a success? Am I not right? And does not the world *now* see it?"[13] What had previously been a hotly stated supposition was now a confirmed fact as far as Sherman was concerned. He would guarantee his military success, if he could keep reporters away.

In March 1864 Sherman took command of the entire Division of the Mississippi when Grant was called east to direct Union fortunes in that theater of the war. The press must have realized that sooner or later something like this would happen, but newsmen still reacted to the news with shock. Where previously they had devoted so much space to the Meridian expedition, now they remained silent on Sherman's promotion. In the days immediately before the announcement, W. F. G. Shanks of the *New York Herald* had supported the appointment of Don Carlos Buell. When Sherman gained the post, Shanks said nothing.[14] The press was obviously unhappy at Sherman's good fortune but apparently decided that the wisest response was silence rather than denunciation. It made no sense to continue to antagonize the man who controlled reporters' fortunes in the entire western theater.

Sherman made no comment on this press silence. He accompanied Grant as far north as Cincinnati, and the two men spent their time together coordinating plans for future military operations. Grant continued on to Washington, while Sherman paid his wife and family a visit. He also received a warning. His Senator brother counseled him to be more careful than ever now that he held such a prominent position. He had to maintain "utter disregard of flattery and clamor."[15] John Sherman worried about his brother's anti-press activities and his recurring attacks on politicians, the Lincoln administration in particular. He must have known that his brother would again ignore his advice, but at least he could feel satisfied that he had tried.

It was obvious that Sherman would not lower his voice simply because he now had a position of increased authority. In the past, the more authority he had had, the more firmly he had acted against his press enemies. The same thing happened again; he quickly took action against newspapers and anyone friendly to them. He wrote a threatening letter to a subordinate he suspected of passing information to reporters. "If my dispatches to you reach the public and the enemy again you will regret it all the days of your life." When he saw a *Louisville Journal* editorial warning of a "general and most formidable invasion of Kentucky," he told the commander there that "rumor and nonsense of that sort" had to stop. He promised to stop it at the front even if he had to "banish all the [newspaper] tribe."[16]

As before, he tried his best to keep his word. While he prepared for his drive against Atlanta, he simultaneously worked to frustrate reporters. He commandeered the railroads between Louisville and Nashville and issued a standing order to keep all "sickly sycophantic meddling" civilians off. If there was any doubt whom he meant, he dispelled it by curtly refusing reporter W. F. G. Shanks's request for a railroad pass and bluntly answering a similar inquiry from the Christian Commission by saying "There is more need of gunpowder and oats than any moral or religious instruction."[17]

Sherman was not convinced that this order would suffice to keep reporters and other unwanted civilians away, so he attempted to gain authority for the ultimate deterrent. He asked the Judge Advocate General for the power to approve the death sentence in the field, arguing that he needed it to counteract spies and guerrillas. He promised justice for all because he believed "the veriest demon should have a hearing and a trial."[18] Fortunately for reporters and southern civilians, Sherman never gained this authority. But the message was clear; Sherman's anti-press fixation, bolstered by the success of the Meridian expedition, had now evolved to the point of attempting to legitimatize his oft-repeated threat to hang reporters as spies. He was firmly convinced that Army victories would be assured if the press was excluded. If the death sentence would insure censorship, it was just as appropriate as any other method.

Sherman began his move against Atlanta on 6 May 1864, the same day Grant began his Wilderness Campaign against Lee in Virginia. Union armies were moving in a coordinated giant pincer movement which would achieve Confederate defeat within one year. Sherman had prepared himself and his army well. He again excluded newsmen, but, once more, several managed to attach themselves, anyway. Still, Sherman imposed such total secrecy on his plans and activities that rumors began circulating that he was even opposed to his Army sending and receiving mail. To clear up this misconception, he issued a circular on 20 May heartily encouraging mail. Unlike later believers in military censorship, he did not include soldiers' mail home as a threat to military secrecy. What he opposed was:

> the maintenance of that class of men who will not take a musket and fight, but follow an army to pick up news for sale, speculating upon a species of information dangerous to the army and to our cause, and who are more used to bolster up idle and worthless officers than to notice the hard working and meritorious whose modesty is generally equal to their courage, and who scorn to seek the cheap flattery of the press.[19]

Most of Sherman's staff, including his brother-in-law Hugh Ewing, disagreed with this circular, while the *Cincinnati Gazette* enunciated general newspaper sentiment by calling it "the most foolish expression that has ever been delivered in all the military fooling with this subject since the war began." Sherman insisted that the circular "was exactly right." He felt its promulgation was probably responsible for the "paucity of news from the army."[20] Until everyone realized that press sensationalism had caused this war and kept it going, fighting would continue. Sherman remained convinced that the complicated civil war had a simple antecedent—the activities and publications of newspaper reporters.

Still, Sherman once more did not display consistency in his anti-press attitude. In June of 1863, the editor of the *Memphis Bulletin* had written him proposing to send reporter De B. Randolph Keim to look after Sherman's journalistic interests. Though such an arrangement violated Sherman's repeated opposition to the practice of generals serving as patrons for reporters in return for good publicity, he surprisingly made no response. Keim did not reach Sherman's area until February 1864, and, by then, he had gained another valuable ally, Sherman's friend and colleague, General James B. McPherson. Keim called on Sherman and mentioned his friendship with McPherson. When they had finished conversing, Keim told Sherman he realized that, since he was a reporter, he would have to leave the area. Sherman feigned surprise: "What are you talking about?" "You are not one of those fellows. You are a volunteer and on McPherson's staff." "Oh yes; beg pardon," gasped the stunned reporter.[21]

Whether Sherman allowed Keim to stay because of the Memphis editor's letter or because of the McPherson connection is uncertain, but unimportant. Despite his oft-stated anti-press position, Sherman was just as willing as any other military man to use reporters to his advantage. He seemed to be saying that he did not dislike correspondents per se; he disliked those who disagreed with him. By allowing Keim to stay, Sherman disobeyed his own exclusion order, and the reporter was able to accompany the Army during the march on Atlanta.

Quickly, Sherman came to regret his generosity. On 23 June 1864 the *New York Herald*, Keim's newspaper, announced the Union's success in deciphering the Confederate signal code. Sherman became furious and ordered General George H. Thomas to discover the culprit. Thomas quickly settled on Keim and suggested he "should at once be executed as a spy." Sherman immediately ordered McPherson to arrest the reporter and deliver him to Thomas for punishment. McPherson asked Thomas for a clarification of Sherman's order, and Thomas surprisingly answered that he "did not know anything about [Keim]" or why Sherman had ordered his arrest. Keim appeared "to be an honest-looking man" and, on McPherson's word, would only be banished from the area for the war's duration.[22] Since this was done, Sherman was satisfied and did not pursue the matter any further. Thomas was either playing military politics, or he was trying to avoid another Knox incident. Fortunately Sherman never discovered his duplicity. In any case, Sherman had learned first hand that even a prominent sponsor did not guarantee a reporter's reliability. His anti-press attitude certainly needed no further encouragement, but this incident provided more.

Other than this self-imposed slip with Keim, Sherman's press restrictions during his Atlanta march were effective. The only information which appeared in northern newspapers was the approximate location of Sherman's army and the announcement that he was having "Splendid Success," "Continued Success," or "Important Successes." Sherman announced captured areas only after he had personally determined sufficient time had elapsed. He responded strongly when further controversy erupted over his exclusion of reporters from the railroads. The railroad's job was to carry army supplies, he bluntly stated. Since newspapers were like any other freight, they could be carried, but "News venders, like any merchants . . . [could] not travel in the cars to sell their goods any more than grocers or hucksters" could. He insisted he was not trying to keep papers from being sold, but continued to believe in the need for laws to punish editors publishing contraband news. Newspapers should publish misleading information, however, and Sherman followed his own advice on more than one occasion during his marches by planting false facts with reporters.[23]

Newsmen were not Sherman's only problems in his determination to keep civilians away from his army and insure its total dedication to its military mission. He also actively continued to oppose the Christian Commission and, in mid-July, he began to protest the presence of state agents recruiting freed slaves for the Union Army. He called such activity "the height of folly," and insisted that the military and not civilians should do it if it was absolutely necessary. He raised such a ruckus that Lincoln personally interceded. Sherman still disagreed, but grudgingly he gave in. In one final act of defiance, he wrote a scorching letter to Massachusetts recruiter John A. Spooner protesting the use of blacks as soldiers.[24]

Sherman's restrictions were so effective that it was two weeks before the press was able to comment on this letter, and they agreed with the general's anti-black sentiment. The *New York Times* called the recruiting of blacks a "delusion." The *New York Herald*, with its rival *Tribune* in strong opposition, praised Sherman's letter for proving that "the abolition theory of equality of races . . . [had] been tested in the fiery ordeal of battle, under the eye of one of the best generals of the day and that it . . . [had] proven a chimera of the flimsiest character."[25]

Sherman expressed surprise over the publication of his letter, asserting that it was actually meant to be ironic. But, to some St. Louis friends, he confided: "I like niggers *well enough* as niggers, but when fools and idiots try and make niggers better than ourselves, I have an opinion." And the opinion was, as he put it later when asked if blacks were not as good as whites in stopping bullets: "Yes, and a sand bag is better; but can a negro [*sic*] do our skirmishing and picket duty? . . . Can they improvise roads, bridges, sorties, flank movements, etc., like the white man? I say no."²⁶

Certainly Sherman was a racist or, as one author later put it, "the nation's most famous unreconstructed rebel."²⁷ The war had not materially changed his prewar proslavery attitude gained while living in the South. To cite one example, his opposition to the Emancipation Proclamation demonstrated, at the least, his lack of antislavery feeling. To be fair, however, Sherman was expressing the common northern opinion of the black man, particularly concerning his incapacity to be a good soldier. The press reaction to his recruiting letter showed he was not out of harmony with public opinion. Sherman's letter raised only a few eyebrows, and these belonged to a minority in the North. The so-called Radical Republicans were sympathetic to the needs and rights of the freed slaves and could not have missed seeing the Spooner letter with its anti-black allusions. They did nothing now, but later would remember these words to Sherman's detriment.

Sherman's philosophy of total war, then, did not include blacks. It did, however, include Confederate noncombatants. During the movement toward Atlanta, his troops destroyed the cotton mills in Roswell Factory (today Roswell), Georgia. Sherman ordered everyone connected with the factory, including hundreds of women, to be transported North. He justified his action on the necessity of thwarting guerrillas whose sniping activities constituted a threat to his army. The only way to neutralize these guerrillas was to eliminate their operational base, the local populace. Sherman saw himself at war not only against the Confederate soldiers but also against every other southerner. This innovation shocked reporters as much as it shocked the rest of the populace, but newspapers expressed their disapproval gingerly. Sherman's anti-press restrictions were too severe to hazard strong criticism. Even safely distant editorial writers said little. Newspapers seemed hesitant to criticize a general moving into the heart of the Confederacy. The *New York Commercial Advertiser* wrote:

> but it is hardly conceivable that an officer bearing a United States commission of Major General should have so far forgotten the commonest dictates of decency and humanity, (Christianity apart) as to drive four hundred girls hundreds of miles away from their homes and friends to seek livelihood amid strange and hostile people. We repeat our earnest hope that further information may redeem the name of General Sherman and our own from the frightful disgrace which this story as it now comes to us must else inflict upon one and the other.[28]

Sherman's continued tight news blackout explains much of this dearth of critical reporting. At times, newspapers had to admit they did not know Sherman's location nor what he was doing. A reporter might only be able to say that he was "not at liberty to particularize" on the Army's progress. Sometimes, desperation drove newspapers to try to guess Sherman's whereabouts, and then the resulting errors were great. On 4 June 1864, for example, the *New York Tribune* quoted the *Washington Republican* in announcing the capture of Atlanta. The *New York Herald* reported the same mistake on 23 July. Newspapers were completely mystified but instead of lashing out at Sherman as they had in the past, they praised him whenever they could discover any hard facts. Even his frontal attack at Kenesaw Mountain, which in the past would have occasioned a recurrence of the insanity charge, now caused little press stir. Newspapers described the Kenesaw repulse as only a minor delay to Sherman's ultimate victory.[29]

When Sherman entered Atlanta on 3 September 1864, the press became ecstatic. Just as this battle was a turning point in the war and in the 1864 presidential election campaign, it was also a turning point in Sherman's relations with reporters. Newspapers became convinced that, despite his anti-press restrictions, Sherman was significantly aiding the Union cause. Bold headlines and fulsome words of adulation announced his defeat of Confederate General Hood at Atlanta. The *New York Tribune* called his action "masterful policy," while the *New York Herald* exclaimed: "Hood Hoodwinked."[30]

The North was overjoyed, and praise poured in from all sides. Quickly, however, controversy replaced congratulations. When Sherman took control of Atlanta, he determined to administer it as a military post. As in Roswell, all civilians would have to leave the city. This order instigated a series of letters between General Hood, Atlanta's mayor and city council, and Sherman. The Confederates accused the Union general of "cruelty," and he responded that "war is cruelty and you can not refine it." He told Atlantans as he had told Halleck sometime earlier that, if southerners wanted to end the hardships of battle, "their relatives . . . [had to] stop the war."[31]

This correspondence received wide circulation and universal praise in the northern press. The *Washington Chronicle* said Sherman was "as trenchant with his pen as [he was] with his sword." The *New York Herald* believed these letters were more important than the campaign itself in stamping him as "one of the great men of the time." Even his perpetual enemies, the *Cincinnati Gazette* and the *Chicago Tribune*, were impressed. The *Gazette* called the evacuation order "like the blast of the war trumpet."[32] Northern newspapers profusely praised their nemesis. Victory made him a hero and stamped his policy as correct.

Sherman had little time to savor his newly found universal acclaim. He was too busy planning his next movement—the march to the sea. Fortified by a series of military successes achieved under the umbrella of total press censorship, Sherman again imposed tight secrecy and complete exclusion of reporters. At first, the news blackout was successful, but, just a week before the Army's scheduled departure, the 8 November 1864 *Indianapolis Journal* discussed the size and plans of Sherman's force. The *New York Times* picked the story up, gave detailed numbers, and predicted that Sherman's destination was either Savannah or Charleston. The Richmond papers reprinted the story soon after.[33]

Sherman became enraged when he learned of this newspaper threat to his forthcoming march's success. He demanded that the War Department arrest the Indianapolis editor and publish misleading information to try to undo the damage. The usually laconic Grant also wrote to Secretary of War Stanton demanding action. Stanton blamed Sherman for the news leak. "If he cannot keep from telling his plans to paymasters, and his staff are [sic] permitted to send them broadcast over the land, the Department cannot prevent their publication."[34] The meaning of Stanton's reference to paymasters is unclear, but obviously he was indicting Sherman for his habit of openly discussing sensitive matters as he mulled them over in his head. Such behavior had proven harmful to his reputation in Kentucky, and Stanton was now blaming it for the publication of vital intelligence.

Grant did not accept Stanton's contention and responded that the source of the information was not in Sherman's Army but among some Army officers in Canada! He promised to seal this leak, but he did not explain how officers in Canada had obtained information on the plans of a Union Army in Georgia, and how that information had then been published in an Indiana paper. Meanwhile, the *Journal* tried to cover up the disclosure by printing false information. The repentant editor escaped punishment; the fact that he was a brother-in-law of the Indiana governor certainly did not hurt. The controversy calmed down as quickly as it had blown up.[35] With the benefit of hindsight, it is obvious that the Confederates did not gain any advantage from their foreknowledge of Sherman's planned revolutionary action; at the time, however, no one could be sure what effect the leak would have.

Despite the disclosure, Sherman stepped off on time, 15 November 1864. Only eight to ten reporters dared accompany the Army. Sherman had issued no new orders, but his previous blasts and his most recent anger over the press leak were still fresh in reporters' minds. Correspondents also realized Sherman would be cut off from outside communication, and it would be difficult if not impossible to get copy back to their papers. Consequently, the scarcity of news accounts was even greater than it had been during the movement on Atlanta. Northern newspapers were forced to clip Confederate papers while simultaneously warning their readers how unreliable the Confederate press was. Sherman's location remained a mystery, and newspapers were usually forced to print "no news from Sherman today." On 19 November the *Chicago Tribune* asked "Where is Sherman?" and the next day the *New York Herald* echoed: "Where Has Sherman Gone?" Even Abraham Lincoln was mystified. One day he asked A. K. McClure if the newsman would not like to know where Sherman was. When McClure expectantly said he certainly would, Lincoln answered: "Well I'll be hanged if I wouldn't myself."[36]

Despite this uncertainty, newspapers were convinced all was going well. In trying to determine where Sherman would emerge on the coast, the *Cincinnati Commercial* expressed the confidence of the northern press and people. "Where ever Sherman pleases to go, we have no doubt he can go."[37] This 13 December 1864 *Commercial* statement was a far cry from the 11 December 1861 article in which this same paper had declared Sherman insane.

On 26 December 1864 all uncertainty and speculation ended; Sherman presented the city of Savannah, Georgia, to Abraham Lincoln as a Christmas present. This imagery caught the national imagination. The *New York Times* headlined: "Sherman's Christmas Present," and the *Chicago Tribune* called him "Our Military Santa Claus." The *Tribune* even compared his march to the "Anabasis and the best efforts of Marlborough, Napoleon, and Wellington."[38] These were strong words for any newspaper to use, but, coming from one of Sherman's most consistent critics, they were startling.

This press adulation did not sway Sherman. In Savannah he allowed the publication of only two newspapers and held the editors "in the strictest accountability." Any wrongdoing would be "punished severely in person & property." Overall, however, the enforcement of press regulations was less severe than it had been on the march. Reporters were able to enter the city without major difficulty and, after the secrecy of the marches, they were happy to know where Sherman was and to be able to publish stories about him. Sherman was so relaxed he was even able to joke about his nemesis. On New Year's Day, when he was toasted as being equal to Hannibal and Caesar, he responded that they were both "small potatoes [compared to him] as they had never read the *New York Herald.*"³⁹

During the movement through the Carolinas in the early months of 1865, jokes were set aside, and Sherman reverted to a tight clamp on newspaper reporters. He was so successful that the *New York Tribune*, to cite just one newspaper, visibly despaired. On 11 March 1865 it told its readers that news from Sherman was "so scarce" that it "welcome[d] the smallest scraps." In mid-March it wrote: "Of course it is a relief to hear anything from Gen. Sherman." By the end of the month, it cried: "Patience! the need for patience will not be long." Still, the *Tribune* managed to publish news Sherman considered harmful. He was trying to avoid a fight with William Hardee and had the Confederate general in the dark. Then Hardee allegedly picked up a *Tribune*, discovered the ploy, and forced the unwanted engagement at Averysboro, North Carolina. Sherman was so angered that, after the war, he refused an invitation to meet Horace Greeley, the *Tribune*'s editor.⁴⁰

Sherman's successful march through the Carolinas, coming immediately after his previous successes, solidified his altered relationship with the press. His attitude toward reporters and newspapers had not changed, but now he had come close to practicing what previously he had only discussed—total exclusion. The most difficult times in his life had come when he had been surrounded by reporters. His greatest triumphs had occurred when he had been most successful in excluding newsmen. The two were combined in his mind; his military successes were the direct result of his success in excluding reporters. He neglected to notice the absence of any hard and fast evidence that the nonpresence of reporters had directly affected his campaigns' results. Sherman had started out with a preconceived notion and then utilized only those facts which proved that same notion. In his own mind, his two marches had completely vindicated the validity of his view that, in war, the First Amendment should be ignored.

Though newspapers and their reporters were controlled by Sherman's restrictions, they exhibited little resentment in print. Their reports seemed to indicate that they were willing to tolerate censorship so long as Sherman was successful. Or perhaps more accurately, they were convinced that new attacks on Sherman would increase rather than solve their problems. Press dislike for the press-hating general had not been dissipated by his success; it was being suppressed. The battle between general and reporters was not over; Sherman's victories had merely produced a truce. Only the future would tell if the truce would become a permanent peace. The Memphis hiatus had not lasted, and this one was even more fragile, so the prognosis for peace was not good.

NOTES

1. *New York Herald*, 22 April, 25, 26, 27, 29 May, 5 June 1863.

2. *Louisville Journal*, 4 July 1863; *New York Tribune, New York Herald, New York Times, Cincinnati Gazette, Louisville Journal, Chicago Tribune*, 8 July 1863.

3. William T. Sherman to U. S. Grant, 4 July 1863, *War of the Rebellion . . . Official Records of the Union and Confederate Armies* (Washington, 1880-1901), Ser. I, 24, pt. 3: 472. Hereafter cited as: *O. R.*

4. Abraham Lincoln to John A. Dix, 8 June 1863, Lincoln, *The Collected Writings of Abraham Lincoln*, ed. Roy P. Basler (New Brunswick, N. J., 1953), 6: 254; WTS to Ellen Sherman, 3 June, 15 July 1863, ES to WTS, 23 June 1863, Sherman Family Papers, University of Notre Dame Archives. Hereafter cited as: S. F. P., UNDA. Father Carrier's diary in manuscript form in UNDA is silent on this subject. *Cincinnati Gazette*, 10 June 1863; *New York Tribune*, 11 June, 9 July 1863.

5. ES Diary, 14 August 1863, S. F. P., UNDA; WTS, *Memoirs of General William T. Sherman* (New York, 1886), 1: 393; WTS to Tommy Sherman, copy, 4 October 1863, WTS to ES, 6 October 1863, S. F. P., UNDA.

6. WTS to Halleck, 4 October 1863, *O. R.*, Ser. I, 30, pt. 4: 73.

7. WTS to S. A. Hurlbut, 26 October 1863, Special Orders No. 264, Hq., 16th Army Corps, 26 October 1863, WTS to D. C. Anthony, 27 October 1863, WTS to Editors of *Bulletin*, 27, 28 October 1863, O.R., Ser. I, 31, pt. 1: 747–748, 750, 764, 766, 848.

8. WTS to J. B. Bingham, 9 November 1863, *O. R.*, Ser. I, 31, pt. 3: 97-98.

9. *New York Herald*, 2 November 1863; Henry Villard, *Memoirs of Henry Villard: Journalist and Financier, 1835-1900* (Boston, 1904), 2: 237–238.

10. WTS to ES, 14 November 1863, ES to WTS, 18 November 1863, ES Diary, 25 December 1863, 1 January 1864, S. F. P., UNDA.

11. WTS to JS, 30 December 1863, William T. Sherman Papers, Library of Congress. Hereafter cited as: WTS Papers, LC.

12. *New York Herald*, 15, 20, 22, 23, 25, 26 February; 2, 3, 7, 14 March 1864.

13. WTS to ES, 10, 12 March 1864, S. F. P., UNDA. Historian Richard M. McMurry says that "Sherman overestimated his accomplishments or underestimated the Confederates' ability to repair the damage that his men had caused." Still, he said, the expedition demonstrated the Confederacy's weakness. Richard M. McMurry, "Sherman's Meridian Campaign," *Civil War Times Illustrated* 14 (May 1975): 31–32.

14. *New York Herald*, 23 March 1864.

15. ES Diary, 20, 22 March 1864, S. F. P., UNDA; Grant, "Preparing for the Campaigns of '64," in *Battles and Leaders of the Civil War*, ed. Robert U. Johnson and C. C. Buel (New York, 1884-1888), 4: 98; JS to WTS, 26 March 1864, WTS Papers, LC.

16. WTS to General Brayman, 2 April 1864, *O. R.*, Ser. I, 32, pt. 3: 231; *Louisville Journal*, 2 April 1864; WTS to General Burbridge, 2 April 1864, *O. R.*, Ser. I, 32, pt. 3: 236–237.

17. WTS to JS, 6 April 1866 [*sic*] WTS Papers, LC; W. F. G. Shanks, *Personal Recollections of Distinguished Generals* (New York, 1866), pp. 21–22; Lemuel Moss, *Annals of the United States Christian Commission* (Philadelphia, 1868), p. 496.

18. WTS to Joseph Holt, 6 April 1864, *O. R.*, Ser. II, 7: 18–19.

19. John E. Hayes to Sydney Howard Gay, 26 February, 8 May 1864, Sydney Howard Gay Papers, Butler Library, Columbia University; Circular, Hq., Military Division of the Mississippi, 20 May 1864, *O. R.*, Ser. I, 38, pt. 4: 272.

20. George W. Pepper, *Personal Recollections of*

Sherman's Campaign . . . (Zanesville, Ohio, 1866), p. 90; *Cincinnati Gazette*, 15 June 1864; WTS to ES, 22 May, 9 June 1864.

21. James Bingham to WTS, 12 June 1863, WTS Papers, LC; De B. Randolph Keim, *Sherman: A Memorial in Art, Oratory and Literature* . . . (Washington, 1904), p. 244.

22. Ibid.: There is no mention of the expulsion nor of any ill-feeling on Keim's part in Keim's favorable account of Sherman's life. J. Cutler Andrews, in *The North Reports the Civil War* (Pittsburgh, 1953), pp. 552–554, felt the disclosure was a mistake. *New York Herald*, 23 June 1864; WTS to George H. Thomas, WTS to J. B. McPherson, McPherson to Thomas, 29 June 1864, Thomas to McPherson, 30 June 1864, *O. R.*, Ser. I, 38, pt. 4: 637, 642. Reporter Cadwallader said: "Sherman could not be greatly blamed for expelling him [Keim] from the army." Sylvanus Cadwallader, *Three Years with Grant*, ed. Benjamin P. Thomas (New York, 1956), pp. 97–98.

23. *New York Herald*, 11, 12, 18, 20 May 1864; *New York Tribune*, 30 May 1864; WTS to General Webster, 20 May 1864, *O. R.*, Ser. I, 38, pt. 4: 262; WTS to General Webster, 4 August 1864, WTS to George H. Thomas, 5 August 1864, WTS to Halleck, 23 August 1864, *O. R.*, Ser. I, 38, pt. 5: 351–352, 363–377, 638; WTS to Charles A. Dana, 10 November 1864, *O. R.*, Ser. I, 39, pt. 3: 727; WTS to Major General Terry, 16 March 1865, *O. R.*, Ser. I, 47, pt. 2: 867.

24. WTS to Halleck, 2 telegrams, 14 July 1864, Abraham Lincoln to WTS, 18 July 1864, WTS to Lincoln, 21 July 1864, *O. R.*, Ser. I, 38, pt. 5: 136-137, 269-270; WTS to John Spooner, 30 July 1864, reprinted in *Chicago Tribune*, 18 August 1864.

25. *New York Times*, 16 August 1864; *New York Herald*, 17 August 1864; *New York Tribune*, 18 August 1864.

26. WTS to Thomas Ewing, 15 September 1864, Ewing

Family Papers, Library of Congress; WTS to William McPherson, ca. September 1864, Collection of W. K. Bixby of St. Louis, privately printed, 1919, William T. Sherman Papers, Henry E. Huntington Library; Lloyd Lewis, *Sherman: Fighting Prophet* (New York, 1932), p. 394.

27. Robert K. Murray, "General Sherman, the Negro and Slavery: The Story of an Unreconstructed Rebel," *Negro History Bulletin* 22 (March 1959): 128; see also Kathleen M. Cresto, "Sherman and Slavery," *Civil War Times Illustrated* 17 (November 1978): 13–21.

28. Hartwell T. Bynum, "Sherman's Expulsion of the Roswell Women in 1864," *Georgia Historical Quarterly* 54 (March 1970): 169–182, but especially 169, 170, 173, 179.

29. *New York Tribune*, 4 June 1864; *New York Herald*, 6, 29 June, 18 July, 5 August 1864.

30. *New York Tribune, New York Herald, Cincinnati Commercial*, 3 September 1864.

31. See, for example, Order of Thanks to William T. Sherman and Others, 3 September 1864, Basler, *Lincoln*, 7: 533; WTS to Halleck, 4 September 1864, *O. R.*, Ser. I, 38, pt. 5: 794; The Sherman-Hood-Atlanta officials correspondence was printed in many newspapers and may also be found in WTS, *Memoirs*, 2: 118–128.

32. *Washington Chronicle*, 23 September 1864; *New York Herald*, 25 September 1864; *Cincinnati Gazette*, 20 September 1864; *Chicago Tribune*, 29 September 1864.

33. Robert S. Harper, *Lincoln and the Press* (New York, 1951), pp. 331–333; *New York Times*, 10 November 1864; James G. Randall, "The Newspaper Problem in its Bearing upon Military Secrecy during the Civil War," *American Historical Review* 23 (January 1918): 331; Henry Hitchcock, *Marching With Sherman*, ed. M. A. DeWolfe Howe (New York, 1927), pp. 100–101.

34. Grant to Edwin Stanton, Stanton to Grant, 11 No-

vember 1864, *O. R.*, Ser. I, 39, pt. 3: 740.

35. Grant to Stanton, 12 November 1864, photostat, U. S. Grant Papers, Library of Congress; Harper, p. 333; Randall, p. 331.

36. It is of more than passing interest that, in 1862, Ellen Sherman had written her husband: "I hope this may not be a war of emancipation but of extermination, & that all under the influence of the foul fiend may be driven like Swine into the Sea. May we carry fire & sword into their states till not one habitation is left standing." ES to WTS, 30 August 1862, S. F. P., UNDA; S. H. M. Byers, *The March to the Sea: A Poem* (Boston, 1896), p. 145n; Andrews, pp. 575–576; *Chicago Tribune*, 19 November 1864; *New York Herald*, 20 November 1864; A. K. McClure, *Abraham Lincoln and Men of War Times* ... (Philadelphia, 1892), p. 216.

37. *Cincinnati Commercial*, 13 December 1864.

38. WTS to Lincoln, 22 December 1864, *O. R.*, Ser. I, 44: 783; *New York Times*, 26 December 1864; *Chicago Tribune*, 26, 28 December 1864.

39. Special Field Orders No. 143, Hq., Military Division of the Mississippi, 26 December 1864, *O. R.*, Ser. I, 44: 813; WTS to ES, 2 January 1865, S. F. P., UNDA.

40. *New York Tribune*, 7, 11, 15, 24 March 1865; WTS, *Memoirs*, 2: 292; Randall, p. 311; Harper, p. 136.

7
Sherman Stumbles

AS SHERMAN AND HIS ARMY plunged ever deeper into the Carolinas, it became obvious that the Confederacy was close to defeat. Grant's and Sherman's giant pincer was closing around the Confederate armies; the Civil War was in its last grim days. Thoughts now began to turn to postwar America: what was going to happen to the defeated rebel states, their government officials, and their people, both slave and free? To consider these questions, the Union high command held a summit meeting. Present on board the "River Queen" anchored at City Point, Virginia on 27-28 March 1865 were the architects of the Union victory: Abraham Lincoln, Ulysses S. Grant, Admiral David Dixon Porter, and William Tecumseh Sherman.

For Sherman this must have been a particularly happy occasion. Any lingering doubts about his being a success were now gone. He was recognized as one of the nation's most prominent military men. If he thought about it that day, he must have recalled earlier unhappy times. He might have remembered his doubts and uncertainties about rejoining the Army and his disgust with the early Union war effort. He might have recalled his emotional difficulties in Kentucky, culminating in the newspaper charge that he was insane. On a happier note, he might have remembered his return to favor at Shiloh, his success in stymying reporters at Memphis, and his subsequent rise to national fame because of his dramatic marches on Atlanta, to the sea, and through the Carolinas. As he sat with his military colleagues and with President Lincoln, he might once again have attributed his military fame to his success in frustrating newspaper reporters. He had accomplished strict press control and could point to his military successes to support his position that total censorship was necessary for victory.

But this was the past, and the conference was concerned with the future. The discussion centered on Union military plans during the next several weeks. Sherman and Grant believed that the war would not end without more bloodshed, but Sherman was confident he could force his opponent, General Joseph E. Johnston, to accept an imposed treaty. Lincoln said he wanted to avoid unnecessary bloodshed and wanted "the most liberal and honorable terms" granted.[1]

Sherman needed little prompting from the President. Often it is still believed that Sherman's only intent in pillaging and destroying was brutalization of the South. Actually, his aim was not to punish but to avoid needless death and suffering by ending the war as quickly as possible. Sherman believed that the South would never surrender unless it became convinced its cause was lost. He regarded his total war campaigns from a psychological point of view; by bringing war's violence home to the populace, he would break southern will, disrupt Confederate Army morale, and thereby hasten the fighting's end. His aim was swiftness and efficiency, not barbarity. At City Point, then, Abraham Lincoln reinforced Sherman's already strongly held desire to end the war as quickly as possible with the least bloodshed. Sherman left the meeting convinced of Lincoln's agreement that any treaty's chief consideration should be mercy and a return to the *status quo ante bellum.*

Sherman returned to his Army in North Carolina and continued pushing Johnston's forces North. Meanwhile, Grant had similar success against Lee, and soon the Confederate general surrendered at Appomattox Court House. Sherman was elated and wrote Grant praising his "Magnanimous and liberal" action. He hoped to offer Johnston similar terms soon.[2]

Several days after Lee's surrender, Johnston asked for a truce so that "further effusion of blood and devastation of property [might be avoided] . . . to permit the civil authorities to enter into needful arrangements to terminate the existing war." Sherman immediately offered Johnston the same terms Grant had offered Lee and reported this fact to Grant and Secretary of War Edwin Stanton. He promised to be "careful not to complicate any points of civil policy."[3]

All seemed to be going well, but then disaster

struck. On the morning of 17 April while Sherman was getting ready to board the train which would take him to Durham Station, North Carolina, for the formal meeting with Johnston, news arrived of Lincoln's assassination. Sherman was shocked but kept the intelligence to himself. As soon as the two generals were alone, however, Sherman showed Johnston the numbing telegram. The Confederate general read the news, and "The perspiration came out in large drops on his forehead, and he did not attempt to conceal his distress. He denounced the act as a disgrace to the Age." Sherman quickly reassured Johnston that he did not suspect any Confederate complicity in the murder, apparently not realizing that many other northerners did or soon would.[4]

Because of the shock over Lincoln's death, no negotiations were conducted that day. When Sherman and Johnston returned to Durham Station the next day, a third person was present, Confederate Secretary of War John C. Breckinridge in his status as a Confederate major general. During the course of the discussions, a messenger arrived with correspondence from Confederate Postmaster-General, John H. Reagan. Among the papers was a surrender proposal. That which had begun as a simple military surrender negotiation modeled on the Grant-Lee talks had changed substantially. The assassination of Abraham Lincoln, the introduction of a Confederate cabinet member as a negotiator, and the discussion of terms submitted by another Confederate official made this meeting more than a military discussion. But Sherman blithely carried on unmindful of the danger. He read Reagan's proposals but found them "inadmissable." He sat down at a table in the farm house and, as he later put it, "recalling the conversation of Mr. Lincoln, at City Point," wrote out terms which he considered "concisely expressed his [Lincoln's] views and wishes." This statement entitled "Memorandum or Basis of Agreement" went well beyond anything Grant and Lee had discussed and included the civil policy Sherman had promised not to negotiate. The terms called for the Confederate Army to disband and then take its arms and store them in state arsenals. An oath of allegiance to the Union was also required. State governments were to be recognized, and Federal courts to be reestablished. All constitutional political rights were to be guaranteed, and no one was to be punished for his part in the war as long as he obeyed the law. "In general terms—the war [was] to cease; [and there was to be] a general amnesty." This was only a tentative agreement, and Washington had to approve before it would go into effect. In the meantime, the *status quo* was to be maintained unless either side gave forty-eight hours notice.[5]

It is difficult to understand why Sherman discussed such terms since they obviously exceeded his competence as a military man. He did not have the authority to negotiate political questions, yet he did so without any indication of concern. In fact, he was certain he was only reflecting Lincoln's ideas. He wrote Johnston of his certitude that the Federal Government would accept the agreement, although he thought clarifications would probably be required. As long as the South acknowledge slavery's demise, its absence in the agreement would not be a problem.[6] As in his anti-press actions, Sherman was convinced he had acted properly and fully expected to receive the nation's gratitude.

The administration in Washington did not receive Sherman's terms with the adulation and joy he felt they deserved. The cabinet was still in shock over Lincoln's death and unanimously rejected the peace terms. They agreed that Sherman had gone beyond his authority; no military man had the right to decide political matters. Stanton was particularly opposed to Sherman's treaty and, after the Cabinet discussion was completed, he ordered Grant to assume Sherman's command and negotiate a new agreement with Johnston. Grant immediately wrote Sherman and said nothing about replacing him, but he informed him that the truce was terminated.[7]

Sherman reacted to the news in characteristic fashion. He called his generals together and "paced up and down the room like a caged lion," letting loose a stream of "furious invective" that stunned the assembled brass. He called Stanton "a mean, scheming, vindictive politician" who robbed military men of their just due. He lambasted his old foes, newspapers and their reporters, reiterating all his familiar arguments against them. Carl Schurz, one of the stunned generals, feared such an outburst might hurt Sherman's reputation, but he felt sure his superior was only blowing off steam. Feelings throughout Sherman's army were high, however; a private, in a letter home, warned that those who called Sherman names would have his Army "to reckon with the first thing they know."[8]

When Grant arrived on 24 April Sherman was still furious, and Grant's first task was to calm him. Despite his orders to relieve Sherman, Grant acted only as a behind-the-scenes adviser. The two men were friends, so Sherman accepted this arrangement, although it is probable he would not have been as cooperative with anyone else.[9]

Following Grant's advice, Sherman repudiated the original agreement, and Johnston surrendered again on 26 April. Grant forwarded the new strictly military agreement to Washington and included a defense of Sherman's original pact. He said that Sherman had simply followed Lincoln's views, the model of the Grant-Lee negotiations, and the precedent of the convocation of the Virginia legislature by General Godfrey Weitzel. (He had not known of the withdrawal of the authority for this Virginia assembly.) Stanton read this letter and then communicated it to the Adjutant General. First, however, he deleted the section favorable to Sherman.[10]

This secret action was but a harbinger of Stanton's public strategy. The Secretary of War had been very upset by Sherman's peace terms from the first. He suspected the general's often expressed anti-black attitude and apparently decided Sherman was a threat to the nation. Stanton probably feared that Sherman, as a popular general, might organize a political party around the peace terms and thus endanger the hard-fought Union victory. In the anxious time after Lincoln's assassination, anything, even a Sherman conspiracy, seemed possible.

Stanton decided to destroy Sherman before he could destroy the nation.

On 23 April 1865 Stanton released Sherman's agreement to the nation's newspapers and attached his reasons for repudiating it; he attributed the worst possible motives to Sherman. When some newspapers mistakenly separated the repudiation from the agreement's text, the War Department sent them a sharp reprimand.[11] Stanton wanted to be certain that the Sherman-Johnston agreement did not receive a favorable audience, and, appropriately, he used Sherman's enemy, the press, to try to achieve his aim.

Stanton's press release took the form of a letter to General John A. Dix and was a blanket indictment of Sherman. It accused the general of overstepping his authority and granting "practical acknowledgement of the Rebel Government." Sherman had tried to resurrect the rebel state governments, Stanton argued, and thus jeopardized the loyal state governments and the new state of West Virginia. His guarantee of property could be interpreted as reestablishing slavery or binding the Federal Government to pay the Confederate debt. Warming to the task Stanton made even more damning allusions. He included in this release a copy of a 3 March letter from Lincoln to Grant prohibiting military negotiations of political matters. By doing this, he gave the erroneous impression that Sherman had seen this letter and had negotiated against Lincoln's wishes. Stanton also argued that one of Sherman's orders relocating troops had opened the way for Jefferson Davis to escape to

Mexico or Europe with a large amount of plunder. In all, Stanton accused Sherman of treason, arguing that his treaty would allow the Confederacy to renew the revolution in the future.[12]

Newspapers printed this sensational statement and quickly began to discuss it. With the exception of Lincoln's assassination, no Civil War news item received as much newspaper coverage as this Sherman-Johnston agreement. It was a major story, it was exciting, and it showed the press's enemy in a bad light. It had all the necessary elements for a newspaper stir.

The press had been full of rumors even before the publication of the Stanton statement or the existence of any hard news on the topic. The *New York Herald*, for example, had prophesied an agreement between Sherman and Johnston a week before it was actually signed. Considering the plight of reporters in Sherman's army, this was a remarkable achievement. Throughout his Carolinas march, Sherman had continued insulting reporters, harassing them, and, most importantly, completely concealing his plans. He refused reporters the use of the telegraph and slowed down or sometimes even stopped the mails. He controlled railroads and steamers. Getting copy to editorial offices was a monumental task for reporters. Elias Smith, of the *New York Herald*, lamented: "A cat in hell without claws is nothing [compared] to a reporter in Gen. Sherman's army."[13]

In this same letter to his editor, reporter Smith also made this more significant statement: "Gen. Sherman *may* be a great General, but he *is* a *great* despot, in my opinion, and a *dangerous man to trust with power.*"¹⁴ These derogatory sentiments were expressed only in a private letter; the *Herald* printed no public attack on Sherman nor against his restrictive policy. Reporters and newspapers did not like what was being done to them, but they were not about to protest in print so long as Sherman kept winning.

This attitude changed when it became apparent that Sherman had committed a major blunder in his negotiations with Johnston. Pent up journalistic frustrations burst forth on 24 April and overflowed into the black bordered issues simultaneously filled with news of Lincoln's death. The press attributed every ill motive possible to Sherman for making his agreement. The important New York papers, the *Times,* the *Herald,* and the *Tribune,* agreed that Sherman's negotiations were a "blind" for Jefferson Davis's escape. The *Washington Star* said the agreement was so favorable to the Confederates that it must have been "adroitly wheedled out of Gen. Sherman by Joe Johnston and the arch conspirators at his elbow." Sherman was "as ignorant and incompetent" at diplomacy as he was accomplished in his field. Even papers generally friendly to Sherman were critical of his agreement. The *Cincinnati Commercial* called the negotiations "an unmitigated mistake," while the *Louisville Journal* expressed "profound sorrow," and the *Washington Chronicle* experienced "amazement." The *Chicago Tribune,* a consistent Sherman critic, used stronger language. It found the terms "painful in the extreme" and blamed them "on the hypothesis of stark insanity."[15] The issue of Sherman's mental balance was again the subject of press discussion.

Newspapers continued their attacks on 25 April, and several more repeated the insanity charge. The *New York Herald* said Sherman had negotiated "under a temporary absence of mind which unfitted him to deal with such shrewd tricksters." The New York *Times* called him "Johnston's outwitted opponent." Surprisingly, the *Chicago Tribune* did not repeat its previous day's insanity accusation and now joined the *St. Louis Missouri Republican* and *Louisville Journal* in demanding that there be no further censure of Sherman until he had had a chance to defend himself. The *Cincinnati Gazette* accused Sherman of disregard for democracy and an attachment to slavery, while the *Washington Chronicle* warned that the public would "submit to no more exhibitions of undeserved mercy to armed traitors."[16]

By 26 April, just two days after word of the agreement had first been published, the press was split into pro and anti-Sherman camps. The pro-Sherman papers included the *Cincinnati Commercial*, the "copperhead" *Cincinnati Enquirer*, the Democratic *St. Louis Missouri Republican*, and George Prentice's *Louisville Journal*. The *New York Herald* and *New York Tribune* drifted into this camp several weeks later. The anti-Sherman papers consisted of those newspapers usually associated with the Radical Republican cause (*Washington Chronicle*, *Chicago Tribune*, *New York Times*, and the *Cincinnati Gazette*). Why the *New York Tribune*, which staunchly espoused Radical Republican issues, did not join in the condemnation of Sherman is unclear.

The two hostile newspaper camps, each one internally and informally united only because of opposition to the Sherman treaty, were soon trying to outdo each other in their battle of words over Sherman's guilt or innocence. The pro-Sherman side agreed that he had made a mistake but argued that his error did not justify impugning his integrity. The *Louisville Journal* argued that Sherman's prior service and his blameless character should have prevented the virulent abuse he was now receiving. The savagery of the attacks proved they originated in something other than the negotiations. The anti-Sherman camp, on the other hand, attributed his actions to ill motives. The *Chicago Tribune* printed rumors that Sherman had become disgusted over being the second man in the army and had "decided to put himself at the head of a pro-slavery party by his generous treaty." The *New York Times* reminded its readers how often in history a victorious general had overthrown a government. In the same breath, however, the *Times* denied believing Sherman had any such coup plans. "As a sane man, he could have had no such purpose."[17]

While his name and reputation were being so freely bandied about, Sherman continued to fume. Stanton's accusations that his negotiations violated Lincoln's orders and aided Jefferson Davis to escape particularly angered him. He denounced the Secretary of War for making the charges and the press for printing them. Before the publication of the

Stanton statement, Sherman had defended his treaty to the Secretary of War by stating: "I admit my folly." After he saw Stanton's letter, he withdrew his confession. "I have no hesitation in pronouncing Mr. Stanton's compilation of April 22 a gross outrage on me, which I will resent in time."[18]

Here was a strange situation indeed. At a time when a hard civil war was at a victorious close, an exclusively Union civil war was beginning. Stanton and Sherman were both impugning each other's integrity, while newspapers took sides. At first glance, the imbroglio seems like a military-civilian confrontation with the newspapers as important allies. However, Sherman also argued the same question with a fellow military man, his former patron Henry W. Halleck. Their dispute shows clearly how much the confusion of the postwar and post-assassination period was responsible for the controversies.

Halleck and Sherman had been friendly since the time "Old Brains" had come to Sherman's defense during the 1861 insanity controversy. They had continued communicating throughout the war, and Sherman had even begun some of his letters with the salutation "My Dear Friend." All this changed when Halleck visited Richmond after Lee's surrender and heard rumors that Jefferson Davis was fleeing South with Confederate specie. Halleck became alarmed and immediately warned Stanton that Davis's scheme included a deal with Sherman or some other Union general. He became so convinced of Sherman's complicity that he tried to thwart the Confederate president's escape plans by ordering all Sherman's subordinates to take orders only from Grant. Halleck became so anxious over this alleged plot that Attorney General Edward Bates described him in his diary as "both knave and fool."[19]

Sherman was already furious because of Stanton's accusations and the press attacks when he learned of Halleck's suspicions. This latest affront caused him to break all ties with Halleck and become insubordinate. Halleck ordered a review of one of Sherman's corps in Richmond, but Sherman refused. When all his troops marched through the Confederate capital, Sherman ignored Halleck watching from his portico and refused to order a salute. He had earlier cautioned Halleck to stay away from his army, warning that he could not guarantee Halleck's safety from the army's anger at "a public insult to a Brother Officer when he was far away on public service, perfectly innocent of the malignant purpose and design."[20]

Sherman's rudeness and insubordination toward a former friend and superior indicated the depth of his anger. One can well imagine his frustration at having his moment of glory ruined by accusations of treason, stupidity, and insanity. His family shared his anger and, as usual, bombarded him with advice. Only John Sherman remained calm. He correctly advised his brother that the administration had disapproved his treaty because it had not contained a statement on slavery. He urged him to ignore Stanton's and Halleck's actions and the newspaper attackers. "The gross damnable perversions of many of the papers and their arraignment of your motives was [sic] more seriously condemned than your arrangements."[21]

Sherman again ignored his brother's counsel of moderation and continued asserting his defense. He wrote several official letters to Grant's adjutant vehemently denying any knowledge of Lincoln's order to Grant until it had appeared in the newspapers. Why was it, he thundered, that "every bar-room loafer in New York . . . [could] read in the morning journals 'Official' matter that . . . [was] withheld from a general whose command . . . [extended] from Kentucky to North Carolina?" He told his wife: "Stanton wants to kill me because I do not favor his scheme of declaring the Negroes of the South, now free, to be loyal voters, whereby politicians may manufacture just so much pliable electioneering material." He also warned Grant against Stanton whom he characterized a "public libeller." In order to maintain his own "self respect" and the support of his men, he felt he had to "resent a public insult."[22]

Sherman had a chance to vent some of his anger when he appeared before the Joint Committee on the Conduct of the War, a solidly pro-Stanton body. The committee sent out a notice of appearance on 5 May, but, for some unexplained reason, Sherman did not receive it until 19 May. In the unsettled atmosphere of Washington, rumors must have spread that Sherman was going to snub the committee, because the *Louisville Journal* felt obliged to print a denial. There is no evidence that Sherman was planning a boycott, but the delay heightened an already tense situation. On 22 May 1865

Sherman appeared before the committee and gave a forceful unflinching performance. He insisted his negotiations reflected Lincoln's ideas and characterized Stanton's and Halleck's actions as unfair. When Stanton had met with him in Savannah in December 1864, he reported, the Secretary of War had encouraged him to deal with civil matters. It was now inconsistent for Stanton to assail him for following this advice. Furthermore, he said, he had never seen Lincoln's order to Grant, Stanton's insinuation notwithstanding.[23]

The encounter was a standoff. Sherman felt he had conducted himself well, and the Committee seemed happy with their actions. Meanwhile, newspapers ignored the whole thing. The *New York Tribune* was one of the few papers to discuss the testimony, and it said that Sherman's statement could be praised or condemned depending on a critic's viewpoint.[24] The nation and the press were less concerned with Sherman's testimony than they were with the huge parade scheduled for the next two days: the Grand Review of the Union Army on 23 and 24 May.

Washington buzzed with preparations for this display of the armed might of the Federal Army, the Union's formal celebration of its victory. Plans called for troops from the eastern theater to pass in review on the first day, while Sherman's army was to receive its adulation on the second. Rumors circulated around Washington that Sherman was planning revenge against Stanton the day of his army's review. Tension filled the air mingling with the exhuberance surrounding the festivities.

Sherman's soldiers roamed the city in the days before the review, and their reputations and Sherman's well-known irascibility made Washington's citizens careful to maintain a discreet silence. The situation was so flammable that the *New York Times*, which had strongly denounced Sherman's agreement, now only meekly hoped that the rumors were inaccurate. John Sherman and Hugh Ewing visited Sherman in his camp and urged him to avoid any rash action. Neither critic nor friend, however, ever expressed any fear that Sherman would attempt a military solution to the imbroglio. He was viewed more as a sulking Achilles than a potential Cromwell.[25]

The review day for Sherman's troops, 24 May, was bright and sunny. Sherman led his army past the main reviewing stand containing the president and high government dignitaries and then, as military custom demanded, dismounted to join them. From a distance, a number of observers trained their field glasses on him and recorded the scene that followed. Accounts varied, but apparently what followed was essentially this. Sherman mounted the stand, saluted the president, and then refused to shake hands with Stanton. In his memoirs, Sherman said he told Stanton: "I do not care to shake hands with clerks." This was the revenge Sherman had threatened, and so many people had feared. The snub happened so quickly that most people never even knew it had occurred. The press was particularly silent, with the *Cincinnati Gazette* alone mentioning it and then only in passing. But, Sherman was satisfied; he had revenged himself on his political tormenter. In later months, his wife tried to mediate the hard feelings, but Sherman refused to shake hands with Stanton until the secretary of war admitted his wrongdoing. Stanton was willing to forgive and forget, but he refused to apologize, and there the matter died.[26]

There is no question but that Sherman had overstepped his authority in negotiating his agreement with Johnston. As an intelligent and experienced military man, he should have known better. His naïveté in never realizing the significance of his action is difficult to explain. He saw a chance to be merciful to a defeated foe, and he took it, never comprehending that both common sense and mercy were required.

Stanton's initial negative reaction was understandable, but his acrimony was unwise. He was correct in feeling Sherman had gone too far, but his insinuation of treason was unfair. Sherman acted improperly, but treason was not the cause; he simply did not understand the ramifications of his act.

Stanton's harsh condemnation can be understood only within the context of the period's confusion. Just as the war was ending, Abraham Lincoln was assassinated, and many believed a Confederate plot was responsible. Jefferson Davis was escaping with what was allegedly an enormous amount of specie, and the rumor circulated, believed by so stolid a man as Halleck, that Sherman was aiding him. During all this confusion and suspicion, Sherman granted terms to a Confederate army which seemed to benefit the South. The immediate reaction of many people was: if Sherman's terms were accepted, the war had been fought for naught. Was the South simply to return to the Union as though nothing had happened? What about slavery, did its absence in Sherman's agreement mean its continuance?

Some of Sherman's earlier statements and actions made this last question particularly significant. His strongly worded anti-black letter protesting the presence of state recruiting agents had received wide circulation, and his opposition to the Emancipation Proclamation was no secret. Henry M. Turner, a black Union army chaplain and postwar religious and political leader, coined the expression *"Shermanized* officer" to describe any army man who shared in what the chaplain called Sherman's "ignoble prejudice." Sherman's anti-black reputation was well known. In December 1864 Halleck had warned him that "a certain class" in Washington felt that his alleged mistreatment of refugee slaves "manifested an almost criminal dislike" toward the "Inevitable Sambo." (At that time Sherman had answered Halleck: "But the nigger? Why in God's name can't sensible men let him alone.") Stanton had earlier become so concerned over Sherman's attitude that on 11 January 1865 he had personally visited Savannah to learn whether the general was protecting black rights. The black leaders he interviewed said Sherman was, but Stanton remained suspicious and so did many others.[27]

Even when Sherman acted favorably toward blacks—the famous Sea Island order establishing former slaves on abandoned plantation lands—he was suspected. The vocal supporter of black rights, the *New York Tribune,* opposed this order and spoke of the "vicious principle of prejudice" which condemned a group of people to isolation simply because of their color.²⁸

Sherman's agreement with Johnston was final proof to Stanton and those who favored the protection of black rights that Sherman posed a threat to this concept. The absence of any mention of slavery and the explicit guarantee of property were read ominously in the context of the past. Sherman seemed to be attempting to make his anti-black attitude part of the basis of the surrender of the last major Confederate army. Since he was a victorious general, one of the nation's heroes, there was always the danger that his ideas might become the basis for a new political party opposed to the protection of the former slaves. Consequently, he had to be suppressed. Accuse him of treason, convince the public through the press that he was cooperating with the Confederates and thus eliminate the danger of his program's acceptance. Sherman's absolute lack of political ambition was never considered. The Sherman-Johnston agreement controversy was not simply a civil-military dispute, therefore; it was one of the first battles of Reconstruction. "The Inevitable Sambo" and his place in the post-Appomattox world was the issue here as it was to be in the Reconstruction years ahead.²⁹

The role of the press is less clear. In issuing his condemnation of Sherman in the press, Stanton was obviously using newspapers to further his designs. Still, the savagery of the initial press attacks indicates that newspapers needed little coaxing.

Newsmen noted that an archenemy had stumbled badly and took the opportunity to gain revenge for the months of harassment and restriction. The pent-up press frustration burst forth because the opportunity presented itself.

Yet as soon as it became clear that a politically motivated attempt was being made to discredit a victorious general, the nearly unanimous newspaper attacks on Sherman ceased. A number of papers began to support the general and defend him against the charges of treason. Newspapers agreed that he had erred (as indeed he had), but they disagreed as to why. Their reports displayed no fondness for Sherman, and the anti-Sherman papers even resuscitated the insanity charge in their attempt to explain his actions. Generally, however, newspapers showed more restraint than might have been expected in light of Sherman's treatment of their reporters and his host of insulting public and private anti-press comments. Sherman had consistently accused newspapermen of aiding the enemy; now he was being accused of the same thing. His reaction to journalists, whom he considered were all threats to national security, was to try to suppress them. Newspaper reaction to his alleged collaboration was at first similarly harsh; but, after making their initial attacks, the newspapers backed off. They did not advocate ignoring the Constitution in order to suppress a military threat to the nation's welfare.

Sherman came out of this encounter with his reputation unscathed. If anything, his treaty blunted his reputation of being a merciless carrier of fire and sword. His image would later revert to that of a wartime destroyer, but, at this time, he remained a popular hero. He was now a success and acknowledged as such, despite the Johnston terms. He had won his battle with reporters; they had not prevented him from helping lead the Union to victory and making himself the success he had so long craved.

NOTES

1. Earl Schenk Miers, ed., *Lincoln Day by Day: A Chronology* (Washington: Lincoln Sesquicentennial Commission, 1960), 3: 323; David D. Porter, *Incidents and Anecdotes of the Civil War* (New York, 1886), pp. 313–315; Porter to William T. Sherman, 1886, cited in WTS, *Memoirs of General William T. Sherman* (New York, 1886), 2: 328–331; WTS to I. N. Arnold, 28 November 1872, Chicago Historical Society.

2. WTS to U. S. Grant, 12 April 1865, *War of the Rebellion . . . Official Records of the Union and Confederate Armies* (Washington, 1880–1901), Ser. I, 47, pt. 3: 177. Hereafter cited as: *O. R.*

3. Joseph E. Johnston to WTS, 14 April 1865, WTS to Johnston, 14 April 1865, WTS to Grant and Secretary of War, 15 April 1865, *O. R.*, Ser. I, 47, pt. 3: 207–208, 221–222.

4. WTS, *Memoirs*, 2: 347–354.

5. Ibid. The text of the memorandum may be found in a number of places including the original in the William T. Sherman Papers, Library of Congress. Hereafter cited as: WTS Papers, LC. It is printed in WTS, *Memoirs*, 2:

356–357 and Joseph E. Johnston, *Narrative of Military Operations* (New York, 1874), pp. 405–407. Johnston's biographers discuss this episode in detail and indicate that Sherman's desire to end the war was his sole motivation. They mention the ensuing Federal controversy over the terms only in passing. Gilbert E. Govan and James W. Livingood, *A Different Valor: The Story of Joseph E. Johnston, C. S. A.* (Indianapolis, 1956), pp. 358–373.

  6. WTS to Johnston, 21 April 1865, *O. R.*, Ser. I, 47, pt. 3: 266.

  7. Gideon Welles, *The Diary of Gideon Welles*, ed. Edgar T. Welles (Boston, 1911), 21 April 1865, 2: 294–295; Benjamin P. Thomas and Harold M. Hyman, *Stanton: The Life and Times* ... (New York, 1962), p. 407; Stanton to Grant, 21 April 1865, Edwin M. Stanton Papers, Library of Congress; Grant to WTS, 21 April 1865, WTS Papers, LC.

  8. Carl Schurz, *The Reminiscences of Carl Schurz* ... (New York, 1908), 3: 114, 116–117; Henry Warner Slocum, "Final Operations of Sherman's Army," in *Battles and Leaders of the Civil War*, ed. Robert U. Johnson and C. C. Buel (New York, 1884–1888), 4: 756; Theodore F. Upson, *With Sherman to the Sea* ... , ed. O. O. Winther (Baton Rouge, 1943), p. 167.

  9. WTS Diary, 24 April 1865, Sherman Family Papers, University of Notre Dame Archives. Hereafter cited as: S. F. P., UNDA. Charles A. Dana, "Reminiscences of Men and Events of the Civil War," *McClure's* 10 (February 1898): 340.

  10. WTS Diary, 25, 26 April 1865, S. F. P., UNDA; Terms of a Military Convention ... , 26 April 1865, WTS Papers, LC; Grant to Stanton, 24 April 1865, *O. R.*, Ser. I, 47, pt. 3: 293; Stanton to John A. Dix, 24 April 1865, quoted in Jacob D. Cox, "Sherman-Johnston Convention," *Scribner's Monthly* 28 (October 1900): 503.

11. Stanton to John A. Dix, 22 April 1865, published in the northern press on 23, 24 or 25 April 1865; see, for example, *New York Herald*, 23 April 1865 and *Washington Chronicle*, 25 April 1865; C. A. Dana to Editors, 25 April 1865, Stanton Papers, LC; Stanton also wrote to one of Sherman's subordinates to be sure he knew of the repudiation of Sherman's terms. Stanton to George H. Thomas, 23 April 1865, *O. R.*, Ser. I, 49, pt. 2: 442–443.

12. Stanton to John A. Dix, 22 April 1865, *New York Herald* 23 April 1865.

13. Ibid., 16 April 1865; Elias Smith to Sydney Howard Gay, 20 April 1865, Sydney Howard Gay Papers, Butler Library, Columbia University.

14. Ibid.

15. *New York Times*, 23 April 1865; *New York Herald, New York Tribune, New York Times, Washington Star, Cincinnati Commercial, Washington Chronicle, Chicago Tribune*, 24 April 1865.

16. *New York Herald, New York Times, Chicago Tribune, St. Louis Missouri Republican, Louisville Journal, Cincinnati Gazette, Washington Chronicle*, 25 April 1865.

17. All of the above newspapers, 26 April-15 May 1865; *Louisville Journal*, 27, 28 April, 1, 2 May 1865; *Chicago Tribune*, 13 May 1865; *New York Times*, 27 April 1865.

18. WTS to Grant, 28 April 1865, *O. R.*, Ser. I, 47, pt. 3: 335; WTS to Stanton, 25 April 1865, Stanton Papers, LC; WTS to John Rawlins, 29 April 1865, *O. R.*, Ser. I, 47, pt. 3: 345.

19. Halleck to Stanton, 22 April 1865, O.R. Ser. I, 47, pt. 3: 277; This letter, of course, must have helped give Stanton the suspicion he wrote into his 22 April 1865 letter to Dix. Stephen E. Ambrose, *Halleck: Lincoln's Chief of Staff* (Baton Route: Louisiana State University Press, 1962), pp. 199–200; Halleck to Stanton, 26 April

1865, *O. R.*, Ser. I, 46, pt. 3: 953–954; Grant, *Personal Memoirs of U. S. Grant* (New York, 1884), p. 651; Edward Bates, *The Diary of Edward Bates: 1839–1866*, ed. Howard K. Beale (Washington, 1933), p. 478.

20. WTS to General Palmer, 4 May 1865, *O. R.*, Ser. I, 47, pt. 3: 399; WTS to ?, 8 May 1865, WTS, *Home Letters of General Sherman*, ed. M. A. DeWolfe Howe (New York, 1909), p. 352; WTS to Grant, 8 May 1865, *O. R.*, Ser. I, 49, pt. 2: 662; Halleck to WTS, 9 May 1865, WTS Papers, LC; *New York Tribune*, 16 May 1865; Leslie Anders, *The Eighteenth Missouri* (Indianapolis: Bobbs-Merrill, 1968), p. 330; WTS to Halleck, 10 May 1865, WTS Papers, LC. According to his major biographer, Halleck's actions were determined by the post-assassination hysteria and by his wishes "to gain Stanton's approval." When he quickly realized that Sherman's friendship meant more to him than Stanton's approval, he apologized to Sherman, but his former friend remained angry. Ambrose, pp. 199–202.

21. ES to WTS, 17 May 1865, S. F. P., UNDA; Thomas Ewing, Jr. to Thomas Ewing, 1 May 1865, Ewing Family Papers, Library of Congress; John Sherman to WTS, 2 May 1865, WTS Papers, LC.

22. WTS to Rawlins, 9 May 1865, *O. R.*, Ser. I, 47, pt. 1: 36; WTS to ES, 10 May 1865, S. F. P., UNDA; WTS to Grant, 10 May 1865, copy, WTS Papers, LC.

23. *Supplemental Reports of the Joint Committee on the Conduct of the War* (Washington, 1866), 1: xxviii–xxxix; *Louisville Journal*, 23 May 1865; *Report of the Committee on the Conduct of the War* (Washington, 1865), 3: 6; *Louisville Journal*, 25 May 1865.

24. *New York Tribune*, 31 May 1865; T. Harry Williams, *Lincoln and the Radicals* (Madison, 1941), p. 381.

25. WTS to S. Van Vliet, 21 May 1865, *O. R.*, Ser. I, 47,

pt. 3: 546–547; C. E. McCartney, *Grant and His Generals* (New York, 1953), p. 299; W. F. G. Shanks, *Personal Recollections of Distinguished Generals* (New York, 1866), pp. 41–42; *New York Times*, 24 May 1865; John C. Arbuckle, *Civil War Experiences of a Foot Soldier* . . . (Columbus, 1930), p. 149.

26. WTS, *Memoirs*, 2: 367, 377; Noah Brooks, *Washington in Lincoln's Times* (New York, 1896), p. 361; Charles A. Dana, *Recollections of the Civil War* (New York, 1898), p. 290; Ben Perley Poore, *Perley's Reminiscences of Sixty Years in the National Metropolis* (Philadelphia, 1886), p. 191; Anonymous, "Recollections of Sherman and Porter," *Nation* 52 (5 March 1891): 192; *Cincinnati Gazette*, 25 May 1865; C. E. McCartney, *Lincoln and His Cabinet* (New York, 1931), p. 349; *Cincinnati Gazette*, 25 May 1865; James M. Merrill, *William Tecumseh Sherman* (New York, 1971), p. 302.

27. Edmund L. Drago, "How Sherman's March Through Georgia Affected the Slaves," *Georgia Historical Quarterly* 57 (Fall 1973): 370; Halleck to WTS, 30 December 1864, *O.R.*, Ser. I, 46: 836; for Sherman's controversial support of a Union general accused of an anti-black atrocity, see James P. Jones, "General Jeff C. Davis, U. S. A. and Sherman's Georgia Campaign," *Georgia Historical Quarterly* 47 (March 1962): 231–248; WTS to Halleck, 12 January 1865, WTS Papers, LC; E. D. Townsend, *Anecdotes of the Civil War* . . . (New York, 1884), pp. 274-275; Josef C. James, "Sherman at Savannah," *Journal of Negro History* 39 (April 1954): 127-137.

28. Willie Lee Rose, *Rehearsal for Reconstruction* . . . (New York, 1967), pp. 325-327; *New York Tribune*, 20, 30 January 1865.

29. Stanton's biographers defend but do not justify the secretary of war's actions. They conclude: "More was involved in this than either man's personal feelings. It

tied in with their differences over policy, with the question of what attitude the government should adopt toward the conquered South and the rights that should be accorded to the Negro." Thomas and Hyman, p. 418.

Conclusion

THE BATTLE between William T. Sherman and newsaper reporters centered on the First Amendment guarantee of freedom of the press. Since this issue had received practically no interpretation in previous years, both sides argued their positions with equal lack of constitutional precedent. The Civil War press believed that the Bill of Rights guaranteed the right to gather and publish news without governmental interference. Only the most blatant journalistic treason could be subjected to any action; normal news activity should be left alone. Newspapermen did not believe that war provided any justification for stifling press criticism and news gathering. The Constitution remained the same in war as in peace. Any attempt to change it was improper.

William T. Sherman did not believe that the Bill of Rights gave the press absolute freedom in peacetime let alone during war. He was convinced that newspaper rights, like the rights of every other

Conclusion

American agency and citizen, had to be subordinated to the military effort. War had to be total, and a highly organized and unified nation had to wage it. Newspapers, like everything else, had to be closely controlled in order to insure maximum war efficiency. Reporters had to be kept away from the army to prevent the publication of even the slightest possible intelligence. Sherman believed the press damaged the war effort. He felt the populace could better understand the military situation by reading soldiers' letters and the reports of army officers. Though he was one of the pioneers of modern total war, Sherman remained the old-line Jominian in this area. War should be conducted by professionals without civilian interference of any kind. Since the Constitution made such military freedom difficult if not impossible, the Constitution had to be set aside for the war's duration. Sherman believed he and his military colleagues should accomplish this constitutional revolution without political or even judicial interference.

During the Civil War, the Lincoln administration adhered to the view that the Constitution remained in effect, and its extraordinary powers allowed the successful promulgation of the war beneath its guidance. Basic civil rights generally remained in effect throughout the war, though they were closely regulated. Despite this fact, Sherman was able to put into practice his view that the First Amendment should be set aside, as he saw fit, during the crisis. His military successes and the idea of military necessity allowed him this significant latitude. Civilian control of the military was not enforced in this major area, and Sherman was able to enforce his anti-constitutional view. In Kaiser-led Germany, in time of war, generals' orders by law superceded civil courts.[1] In the Civil War, Sherman's orders superceded the civilian government's constitutional philosophy without benefit of law. In his own mind, Sherman's actions were not extralegal; they were part of his duty to the nation and thus an essential form of patriotism.

A closer look at Sherman's attitudes, as this study has attempted to do, shows that altruism was not his primary motivation. The vehemence of his anti-press statements and actions shows clearly that Sherman's position resulted more from his personality and past experiences than from a philosophical patriotism. His activities indicate how much nonconstitutional factors determined a seemingly obvious constitutional issue.

Sherman's battle with reporters shows that grave danger exists to freedom of the press any time such a powerful public figure is able to put his anti-press ideas into practice. The First Amendment, like the entire Bill of Rights, is fragile. During war, the call for order and unanimity highlights this fragility even more. There are no set guidelines or conclusive constitutional agreements on how press rights in war differ from those in peace. Consequently, repression is a greater possibility. Sherman's attitudes and practices during the Civil War are only the most obvious manifestations of a recurring movement toward repression in past wars and a warning for any future conflict.

In war, there is common agreement that military

secrets have to be protected; no one maintains that the First Amendment allows the publication of vital information which would endanger the nation's survival. Yet, considering the pressure for censorship which quickly develops in war, the First Amendment's preservation requires that care be taken to insure that any system of censorship be as minimal as possible. Any such system should protect vital military secrets but not impinge on legitimate criticism. An anti-press society like the one envisioned by Sherman and some others who have followed him would not only safeguard real and alleged secrets, but it would also eliminate a basic American right. Ironically, in fighting in the name of American liberties, persons like Sherman take actions that could result in the destruction of those very liberties.

In the years since the Civil War, the Supreme Court has said little about the press in wartime, but it has clearly indicated that the Constitution can not be set aside. Regulation within Constitutional guarantees, not suppression without the document, is the law of the land. As historian James G. Randall has said, however: "The ideal is never realized . . ."; the United States is both a nation of laws and of men.[2] The laws enforcing the First Amendment in war are not definitive, but men like Sherman tend to be. The realization of the ideal of rule of law has consequently always been under seige and no doubt will continue to be in the future.

NOTES

1. James G. Randall, *Constitutional Problems Under Lincoln*, rev. ed. (Urbana, 1951), p. 25.
2. Ibid., p. 513.

Bibliographical Note

This book is based primarily on manuscript sources: the papers of the major persons involved and a representative sampling of leading contemporary newspapers. The following manuscript collections were particularly important: the William T. Sherman Papers in the Library of Congress, in the Henry E. Huntington Library, and in the Ohio Historical Society; and the Sherman Family Papers, in the University of Notre Dame Archives. The latter have been used only in a few recent works. They provided the best insight into Sherman's feelings, consisting as they do of letters to and from Sherman, his wife, and other members of the Sherman and Ewing families. Other collections important to this research were the papers of Simon Cameron, Charles A. Dana, Thomas Ewing, the Ewing family, U. S. Grant, David Dixon Porter, John Sherman, and Edwin Stanton, all in the Library of Congress. The Sydney Howard Gay Papers, Butler Library, Columbia University; a William T. Sherman letter in the Chicago Historical Society; and the Thomas Knox Court-Martial transcript in Records of the Judge Advocate General (Army), National Archives and Records Service, Washington were also essential.

The following newspapers were consulted for the entire Civil War period: *Chicago Tribune;* three Cincinnati papers: *Commercial, Enquirer,* and *Gazette; Louisville Journal;* three New York papers: *Herald, Times,* and *Tribune*; two St. Louis papers:

Missouri Democrat and *Missouri Republican;* and two Washington papers: *Chronicle* and *Star.* Two Memphis, Tennessee, papers, the *Bulletin* and the *Appeal,* were searched for the period from 1 June to 31 December 1862, the approximate time of Sherman's tenure in that city.

As is well known, there is a veritable mountain of printed material on the Civil War: diaries, memoirs, letters of contemporaries and participants, and professional and amateur monographs and journal articles. In the course of researching this book, an attempt was made to consult all the pertinent material, but only those sources found to be most significant will be mentioned here.

Of the printed material, the *War of the Rebellion . . . Official Records of the Union and Confederate Armies,* 128 vols., 1880-1901, was indispenable. Next in importance were memoirs and diaries, the most frequently consulted of which were: David P. Conyngham, *Sherman's March Through the South,* 1865; Henry Hitchcock, *Marching with Sherman,* ed. M. A. DeWolfe Howe, 1927; Joseph E. Johnston, *Narrative of Military Operations,* 1874; Thomas W. Knox, *Campfire and Cottonfield,* 1865; A. K. McClure, *Abraham Lincoln and Men of War Times,* 1892, and *Colonel Alexander K. McClure's Recollections of Half a Century,* 1902; David D. Porter, *Incidents and Anecdotes of the Civil War,* 1886; J. Whitelaw Reid, *Ohio in the War,* 2 vols., 1893; Albert D. Richardson, *Secret Service: The Field, the Dungeon and the Escape,* 1865; W. F. G. Shanks, *Personal Recollections of Distinguished Generals,* 1866; *Memoirs of General William T. Sherman,* 2 vols., rev. ed.,

1886; *Memoirs of Henry Villard: Journalist and Financier, 1835-1900*, 2 vols., 1904; Franc B. Wilkie, *Pen and Powder*, 1888, and *Thirty-Five Years in American Journalism*, 1891. The various printed collections of Sherman letters were also carefully combed, but in many cases they were found to be inaccurate when compared to the original manuscripts.

During the post-Appomattox period, participants in the war published defenses of their own conduct and their opinions of other participants. Many of these remembrances have been gathered together in Robert Underwood Johnson and Clarence Clough Buel (eds.) *Battles and Leaders of the Civil War*, 4 vols., 1884-1888. Magazines containing these memoirs include: *Century, Cosmopolitan, Harper's, Independent, McClure's, North American Review,* and *Scribner's*. The articles of most interest to this book were: Jacob D. Cox, "Sherman-Johnston Convention," *Scribner's Monthly* 28 (October 1900): 489-505; Murat Halstead, "Recollections and Letters of General Sherman," *Independent* 51 (15 June 1899), 1610-1613, (22 June 1899), 1682-1685; Joseph E. Johnston, "My Negotiations with General Sherman," *North American Review* 143 (August 1886): 183-197; W. F. G. Shanks, "Recollections of W. T. Sherman," *Harper's New Monthly* 30 (April 1865): 640-646; W. T. and John Sherman, "Letters of Two Brothers," ed. Rachel Ewing Sherman, *Century*, 45 (November 1892, March, April 1893), 88-101, 425-440, 689-699, 892-903; Henry Villard, "Army Correspondence: Its History," *Nation* 1 (20, 27 July, 3 August 1865): 79-81, 114-116, 144-146.

More recently, letters, remembrances, and diaries

of Civil War participants have been published in historical journals. (The most popular topic seems to be Vicksburg. One might facetiously observe that the length of the siege was due to more diaries being kept than shovels used or bullets fired.) Two of the most useful modern publications were: Rufus J. Mead, "With Sherman Through Georgia and the Carolinas: Letters of a Federal Soldier," ed. James A. Padgett, *Georgia Historical Quarterly* 32 (December 1948): 284-322 and 33 (March 1949): 49-81; Vett Noble, "Vett Noble of Ypsilanti: A Clerk for General Sherman," ed. Donald W. Disbrow, *Civil War History* 14 (March 1968): 15-39.

A number of books on reporters and newspapers proved especially useful. The best study of northern journalism during the Civil War is J. Cutler Andrews, *The North Reports the Civil War* (Pittsburgh: University of Pittsburg Press, 1953). Less comprehensive but helpful were Bernard A. Weisberger, *Reporters for the Union* (Boston: Houghton-Mifflin, 1953), and Louis M. Starr, *Bohemian Brigade: Civil War Newsmen in Action* (New York: Knopf, 1954). Of less value because of a number of inaccuracies was Emmet Crozier, *Yankee Reporters: 1861-1865* (New York: Oxford University Press, 1956). Frank Luther Mott, *American Journalism: A History, 1690-1960*, 3rd ed. (New York: MacMillan, 1962), is still valuable as is Edwin Emery, *The Press and America: An Interpretative History of the Mass Media*, 3rd ed. (Englewood Cliffs, New Jersey: Prentice-Hall, 1972).

Particularly helpful monographs on more specific topics include: Thomas H. Baker, *The Memphis*

Commercial Appeal (Baton Rouge: Louisiana State University Press, 1971); John G. Barrett, *Sherman's March Through the Carolinas* (Chapel Hill: University of North Carolina Press, 1956); Robert S. Harper, *Lincoln and the Press* (New York: McGraw Hill, 1951); Lowell H. Harrison, *The Civil War in Kentucky* (Lexington: University Press of Kentucky, 1975); Harold M. Hyman, *A More Perfect Union: The Impact of the Civil War and Reconstruction on the Constitution* (New York: Knopf, 1973); James L. McDonough, *Shiloh: In Hell Before Night*, (Knoxville: University of Tennessee Press, 1977); James G. Randall, *Constitutional Problems Under Lincoln*, rev. ed. (Urbana: University of Illinois Press, 1951); James G. Smart, ed., *A Radical View: The "Agate" Dispatches of Whitelaw Reid, 1861-1865* (Memphis: Memphis State University Press, 1976); Wiley Sword, *Shiloh, Bloody Shiloh* (New York: William Morrow, 1974); Benjamin P. Thomas and Harold M. Hyman, *Stanton: The Life and Times of Lincoln's Secretary of War* (New York: Knopf, 1962).

Among the numerous Sherman biographies, Lloyd Lewis, *Sherman: Fighting Prophet* (New York: Harcourt Brace, 1932), is still the best study though Lewis did not have the benefit of recently available manuscripts. B. H. Liddell Hart, *Sherman: Soldier, Realist, American* (New York: Harcourt Brace, 1958) has some valuable insights, but it is dated. The latest biography, *William Tecumseh Sherman* by James M. Merrill (Chicago: Rand McNally, 1971), is meant to be a study of the general's personal life. It presents some new points, but it leaves much about Sherman unsaid. John Bennett Walters, *Merchant of Terror: General Sherman and Total War* (Indianapolis: Bobbs-Merrill, 1973), is the publication of Dr. Walters' 1947 doctoral dissertation with a new title and preface. It lacks objectivity and is dated. Anna McAllister, *Ellen Ewing: Wife of General Sherman* (New York: Benzinger, 1936), is unobjectively biased toward Ellen and thus of little use to the historian. Joseph T. Durkin, *General Sherman's Son* (New York: Farrar, Straus and Cudahy, 1959) is more valuable for the period after the Civil War. Paul E. Steiner's sketch of Sherman in *Medical-Military Portraits of Union and Confederate Generals* (Philadelphia: Whitmore Publishing Co., 1968), is not based on manuscript sources and therefore of limited value. T. Harry Williams' account of Sherman in *McClellan, Sherman and Grant* (New Brunswick, New Jersey: Rutgers University Press, 1962), is brief but well done. Most other books about Sherman are limited by their almost exclusive reliance on his memoirs and little else. A recent publication: Mills Lane (ed.) *War is Hell! William T. Sherman's Personal Narrative of His March Through Georgia* (Savannah: The Beehive Press, 1974), consists of excerpts from Sherman's memoirs and letters to his wife. Its introduction and photographs are interesting, but the book's justification is unclear. Richard Wheeler, *We Knew William Tecumseh Sherman* (New York: Crowell, 1977) is another of the author's "eyewitness" books meant for popular consumption. The host of nineteenth-century biographies, though dated and not always historically objective, were found to provide some useful information.

In understanding the problem of press-military

relationships in particular and First Amendment freedoms in general, the following books proved to be the most helpful: Lucius J. Barker and Twiley W. Barker, Jr., *Civil Liberties and the Constitution, Cases and Commentaries*, 3rd ed. (Englewood Cliffs, New Jersey: Prentice Hall, 1979); Zechariah Chafee, Jr., *Government and Mass Communications*, reprinted (Hamden, Conn.: Archer, 1965), and *Free Speech in the United States* (Cambridge: Harvard University Press, 1941); Bruce E. Fein, *Significant Decisions of the Supreme Court: 1975-1976 Term*, (Washington: American Enterprise Institute for Public Policy Research, 1977); William A. Hachten, *The Supreme Court on Freedom of the Press: Decisions and Dissents* (Ames, Iowa: Iowa State University Press, 1968); William E. Hocking, *Freedom of the Press: A Framework of Principle* (Chicago: University of Chicago Press, 1947); Edward G. Hudon, *Freedom of Speech and Press in America* (Washington: Public Affairs Press, 1963); Alfred H. Kelly and Winifred A. Harbison, *The American Constitution*, 4th ed., (New York: Norton, 1970); Milton R. Konvitz, *First Amendment Freedoms* (Ithaca: Cornell University Press, 1963); Theodore F. Koop, *Weapon of Silence* (Chicago: University of Chicago Press, 1946); John Lofton, *Justice and the Press* (Boston: Beacon, 1966); Dale Minor, *The Information War* (New York: Hawthorne, 1970); James R. Mock, *Censorship 1917* (Princeton, New Jersey: Princeton University Press, 1941); Harold L. Nelson (ed.) *Freedom of the Press from Hamilton to the Warren Court*, (Indianapolis: Bobbs-Merrill, 1967); James E. Pollard, *The Presidents and the Press*, (New York: MacMillan, 1947);

Lucy B. Salmon, *The Newspapers and Authority* (New York: Oxford University Press, 1923); Culver Smith, *The Press, Politics and Patronage: The American Government's Use of Newspapers, 1789-1875* (Athens, Georgia: University of Georgia Press, 1977); Frank Thayer, *Legal Control of the Press* (Brooklyn: Foundation Press, 1944); William Whiting, *War Powers Under the Constitution*, 43rd ed., 1871; Stanley N. Worton (comp.), *Freedom of Speech and Press, American Issues in Perspective: A Documentary Approach* (Rochelle Park, New Jersey: Hayden Book Co., 1975). Also important were the published opinions and decisions of the United States Supreme Court.

The following historical journals were particularly helpful: *Civil War History, Civil War Times Illustrated, Georgia Historical Quarterly,* Illinois State Historical Society *Journal, Journal of Mississippi History, Journal of Southern History, Journalism Quarterly,* Kentucky State Historical Society *Register, Military Affairs, Mississippi Valley Historical Review* (now named the *Journal of American History*), *Missouri Historical Review, North Carolina Historical Review, South Atlantic Quarterly.* Some of the more important articles were: "American Press and the Law," *Economist* 63 (2 April 1977): 37-45; "Comments: *United States* v. *Progressive:* The National Security and Free Speech Conflict," 22 *William and Mary* 141 (1980); Stephen E. Ambrose, "William T. Sherman: A Reappraisal," *American History Illustrated* 1 (January 1967): 4-12; Charles H. Brown, "Press Censorship in the Spanish American War," *Journalism Quarterly* 42 (Autumn 1965);

581-590; Hartwell T. Bynum, "Sherman's Expulsion of the Roswell Women in 1864," *Georgia Historical Quarterly* 54 (March 1970): 169-182; Albert Castel, "The Life of a Rising Son [W. T. Sherman]," *Civil War Times Illustrated* 18 (July 1979): 4-7, 42-46 (August): 12-22 (October): 10-21; E. Merton Coulter, "Sherman and the South," *North Carolina Historical Review* 8 (January 1931): 41-54, reprinted in *Georgia Historical Quarterly* 15 (March 1931): 1-18; Kathleen M. Cresto, "Sherman and Slavery," *Civil War Times Illustrated* 17 (November 1978): 13-21; Edmund L. Drago, "How Sherman's March Through Georgia Affected the Slaves," *Georgia Historical Quarterly* 57 (Fall 1973): 361-375; Otto Eisenschiml, "Sherman, Hero or War Criminal?" *Civil War Times Illustrated* 2 (January 1964): 7-9, 29-36; Lowell H. Harrison, "The Civil War in Kentucky: Some Persistent Questions," Kentucky State Historical Society *Register* 76 (January 1978): 1-21; Josef C. James, "Sherman at Savannah," *Journal of Negro History* 39 (April 1954): 127-137; James P. Jones, "General Jeff C. Davis, U. S. A. and Sherman's Georgia Campaign," *Georgia Historical Quarterly* 47 (March 1962): 231-248; Cedric Larson, "Censorship of Army News during the World War, 1917-1918," *Journalism Quarterly* 17 (December 1940): 313-323; B. H. Liddell Hart, "Sherman—Modern Warrior," *American Heritage* 13 (August 1962), 21-23, 102-106; John F. Marszalek, "William T. Sherman and the Verbal Battle of Shiloh," *Northwest Ohio Quarterly* 42 (Fall 1970): 78-85, and "The Stanton-Sherman Controversy," *Civil War Times Illustrated* 9 (October 1970): 4-12, and "The Knox Court-Martial: W. T. Sherman Puts the Press on Trial (1863)," *Military Law Review* 59 (Winter 1973): 197-214; Richard M. McMurry, "Sherman's Meridian Campaign," *Civil War Times Illustrated* 14 (May 1975): 24-34; Robert C. Miller, "Censorship in Korea," *Nieman Reports* 6 (July 1952): 3-6; Robert K. Murray, "General Sherman, the Negro and Slavery: The Story of an Unreconstructed Rebel," *Negro History Bulletin* 22 (March 1959): 125-130; Raoul S. Naroll, "Lincoln and the Sherman Peace Fiasco—Another Fable?" *Journal of Southern History* 20 (November 1954): 459-483; Jack E. Orwant and John Ullmann, "Pentagon Officers' Attitudes on Reporting Military News," *Journalism Quarterly* 51 (Autumn 1974): 463-469; Joseph H. Parks, "Memphis Under Military Rule, 1862-1865," East Tennessee Historical Society *Publications* 14 (1942): 31-58; Harry W. Pfanz, "The Surrender Negotiations between General Johnston and General Sherman, April 1865," *Military Affairs* 16 (Summer 1952): 61-70; James G. Randall, "The Newspaper Problem in its Bearing upon Military Secrecy during the Civil War," *American Historical Review* 23 (January 1918): 303-323; Joe Skidmore, "The Copperhead Press and the Civil War," *Journalism Quarterly* 16 (December 1939): 345-355; John B. Spore, "Sherman and the Press," *Infantry Journal* 63 (October through December 1948): 28-32, 31-35, 30-35; John Bennett Walters, "General William T. Sherman and Total War," *Journal of Southern History* 14 (November 1951): 447-480; Earl Warren, "The Bill of Rights and the Military," 37 *New York University Law Review* 181 (1962).

There are a number of masters theses and doctoral dissertations which deal with aspects of Sherman's career or the Civil War press. They include: Frederic F. Endres, "The Northern Press and the Civil War: A Study in Editorial Opinion and Government, Military and Public Reaction," doctoral dissertation, University of Maryland, 1975; Charles D. Firebaugh, "General William T. Sherman's Attitude Toward the Newspaper Press, 1861-1865," masters thesis, Ohio State University, 1958; Thomas H. Guback, "Control and Censorship of the Northern Press during the Civil War," bachelors thesis, Rutgers University, 1958; Dana F. Kellerman, "Censorship of the Northern Press during the Civil War," masters thesis, University of Illinois, 1960; John F. Marszalek, Jr., "W. T. Sherman and the Press, 1861-1865," doctoral dissertation, University of Notre Dame, 1968; Robert K. Murray, "Sherman, Slavery and the South," masters thesis, Ohio State University, 1947; Craig Tenney, "Major General A. E. Burnside and the First Amendment: A Case Study of Civil War Freedom of Expression," doctoral dissertation, Indiana University, 1977; John Bennett Walters, "General W. T. Sherman and the Philosophy of Total War: A Rehearsal," masters thesis, Vanderbilt University, 1945, and "General William T. Sherman and Total War," doctoral dissertation, Vanderbilt University, 1947.

Bibliographical Note Addendum

The years since the original (1981) publication of this book have seen a veritable explosion in writings on William T. Sherman. A host of theses and dissertations on the matter of the media in time of war have appeared, as have books, articles, columns in contemporary newspapers, and segments on television programs.

It would be beyond the scope of this bibliography to list even a small percentage of these publications, especially those on the legal and political aspects of the issue. Since I found theses, dissertations, and books to be particularly helpful in my attempt to summarize what had happened since 1981 in political-military-media relations, I will mention a number of these. And, since this book focuses on the activities of William T. Sherman, I want to alert the reader to the most significant recent monographs on him. None of the new publications delve into his anti-journalism activities with the depth of this book, so its republication in paperback form will continue to fill what would otherwise be a void in the literature.

A number of biographies of Sherman have appeared in recent years. These include this author's *Sherman, A Soldier's Passion for Order* (New York: Free Press, 1993), the book cited as the new standard life of the general; Michael Fellman, *Citizen Sherman* (New York: Random House, 1995), a sharply critical view of the man; Stanley P. Hirshon, *The White Tecumseh* (New York: John Wiley, 1997), a sympathetic version which leaves much unsaid; Charles Edmund Vetter, *Sherman, Merchant of Terror, Advocate of Peace* (Gretna, La.: Pelican, 1992) and Mark Coburn, *Terrible Innocence: General Sherman at War* (New York: Hippocrene, 1993), brief accounts based primarily on secondary sources.

Then, there are books on Sherman's warfare: Charles Royster, *The Destructive War: William Tecumseh Sherman, Stonewall Jackson, and the Americans* (New York: Oxford University Press, 1991), an attempt to place Sherman's waging of war within the context of changed perceptions of warfare; Mark Grimsley, *The Hard Hand of War, Union Military Policy Toward Southern Civilians 1861-1865* (New York: Cambridge University Press, 1995), a description of the discriminating nature of Sherman's destructive methods; Joseph T. Glatthaar, *The March to the Sea and Beyond: Sherman's Troops in the Savannah and Carolinas Campaigns* (New York: New York University Press, 1985), an analysis of the attitudes of Sherman's soldiers; Lee Kennett, *Marching Through Georgia: The Story of Soldiers & Civilians During Sherman's Campaigns in Georgia* (New York: Harper, 1995), a detailed sympathetic account of the impact of the Atlanta Campaign and the march to the sea on Sherman's soldiers and on Southern civilians; Albert Castel, *Decision in the West: The Atlanta Campaign of 1864* (Lawrence: University Press of Kansas, 1992), which is critical of Sherman's generalship; David Evans, *Sherman's Horsemen: Union Cavalry Operations in the Atlanta Campaign* (Bloomington: Indiana

University Press, 1996), a detailed description of cavalry operations around the city of Atlanta; Joseph H. Ewing, *Sherman at War* (Dayton, Ohio: Morningside, 1992), a collection of Sherman's letters to a relative expressing, as only Sherman could, his perception of the war and his animosity toward reporters; Cynthia Bass, *Sherman's March: A Novel* (New York: Villard, 1994), a novel that exemplifies historical fiction at its best.

In addition to the material cited in the original bibliography, the following theses, dissertations, books, articles, and papers were helpful in summarizing modern political-military-media relationships and constitutional opinion. Dissertations consulted include: Morgan David Arant, "Constitutional Implications of United States Government Restrictions on the Press in the Persian Gulf War," University of North Carolina at Chapel Hill, 1994; Terrance M. Fox, "The Media and the Military: An Explanatory Theory of the Evolution of the Guidelines for Coverage of Conflict," Florida State University, 1995; Susan Sullivan Lagon, "The First Amendment versus National Security: Judicial Interpretations of the Prior Restraint Doctrine," Georgetown University, 1992.

Masters' theses consulted are: Shannon E. Crabtree, "Guidelines for Journalists in Future Military Conflicts," University of Houston, 1995; Leta Yvonne Deyerle, "A Public Relations Model for the Department of Defense during Combat Contingencies," Ohio State University, 1990; Timothy H. Hoyle, "Defending the News Media's Right of Access to the Battlefield," Michigan State University, 1996; David Wayne

Lynch, "Twentieth Century Military-Media Relations: Censorship, Openness, Exclusion and Control," University of Tulsa, 1996; Debra Lynn Pressley, "Us Versus Them: A Survey of Army Public Affairs Officers and the Press," University of Tennessee, Knoxville, 1991; Mark Hillel Samisch, "Comparison of the Media Coverage of the Vietnam War to the Media Coverage of the Invasions of Grenada and Panama: A Question of Legacies," University of Maryland at College Park, 1991; Gary W. Sheftlick, "Airwaves of Intelligence: Content Analysis of 'Desert Storm' Network News," University of South Carolina, 1994.

Among the books consulted are: American Bar Association, *A Journalist's Primer on Freedom of Speech* (Chicago: American Bar Association, 1992); Frank Aukofer and William P. Laurence, *America's Team, the Odd Couple: A Report on the Relationship Between the Media and the Military* (Nashville: Freedom Forum First Amendment Center at Vanderbilt University, 1995); Ted Galen Carpenter, *The Captive Press: Foreign Policy Crises and the First Amendment* (Washington D.C.: Cato Institute, 1995); Henry Cohen, *Press Restrictions in the Persian Gulf War: First Amendment Implications* (Washington, D.C.: Congressional Research Service, Library of Congress, 1991); Pascale Combelles-Siegel, *The Troubled Path to the Pentagon's Rules on Media Access to the Battlefield: Grenada to Today* (Carlisle Barracks, Pa.: Strategic Studies Institute, U.S. Army War College, 1996); Robert E. Denton, ed., *The Media and the Persian Gulf War* (Westport, Conn.: Praeger, 1993); Bradley Greenberg and Walter Garty, *Desert Storm and the Mass Media* (Cresskill, N.J.: Hampton, 1993); Michael Linfield,

Freedom Under Fire: U.S. Civil Liberties in Times of War (Boston, Mass.: South End, 1990); John R. MacArthur, *Second Front: Censorship and Propaganda in the Gulf War* (Berkeley: University of California Press, 1993); Jacqueline E. Sharkey, *Under Fire: U.S. Military Restrictions on the Media from Grenada to the Persian Gulf* (Washington, D.C.: Center for Public Integrity, 1991); Peter R. Young, ed., *Defence and the Media in Time of Limited War* (Portland, Ore.: Frank Cass, 1992).

Articles and papers consulted include: Margaret A. Blanchard, "Free Expression and Wartime: Lessons from the Past, Hopes for the Future," *Journalism Quarterly* 69 (Summer 1992): 5-17; Sandra H. Dickson, "Understanding Media Bias: The Press and the U.S. Invasion of Panama," *Journalism Quarterly* 71 (Winter 1994): 809-819; Caroline Dow, "Prior Restraint on Photojournalists," *Journalism Quarterly* 64 (Summer-Autumn 1987): 88-93, 118; David Lamb, "Pentagon Hardball: Military Restrictions on Press Coverage of Operation Desert Storm," *Washington Journalism Review* 13 (April 1991): 33-36; Elliot Mincberg, "A Look at Recent Supreme Court Decisions: Judicial Prior Restraint and the First Amendment," *Hastings Law Journal* 44 (April 1993): 871-879; Jeffery A. Smith, "The Sword is Mightier Than the Pen: The Lack of Constitutional Authority For Military Restrictions on the Press," paper presented to annual convention of Association for Education in Journalism and Mass Communication, Kansas City, 1993.

Index

Abrams v. *U.S.*, 5
Alien and Sedition Acts, 4–5
American Civil Liberties Union (ACLU), 9, 11
Anderson, Robert, 66, 68–71
Arkansas Post, capture of, 139, 141, 148
Army of the Potomac, 14, 148
Army of the Tennessee, 171
Arnett, Peter, 30
Atlanta, march on, 177–86, 198

Baltimore, Md., 14, 169
Banks, Nathaniel, 131, 135
Bill of Rights. *See* First Amendment
Blackmun, Harry, 6–7
Blacks, 52, 211, 223n (*see also* Slaves); Sherman's bias against, 182–83, 215–16
Blair, F. P., Jr., 134, 141–43, 147
Blair, Montgomery, 15
Breckinridge, John C., 200
Brennan, William, 6
Browne, Junius H., 133, 158
Buckner, Simon, 69, 79
Buell, Don Carlos, 70, 76, 102n, 176
Bull Run, Battle of, 65, 82, 98
Burnside, Ambrose, 17, 56, 174
Bush, George, 25

Cadwallader, Sylvanus, 194n
Cairo, District of, 87–89
Cameron, Simon, 14, 17, 55, 73–76, 80
Casey, James, 48–49
Censorship. *See* First Amendment
Charleston, 40, 186
Chattanooga, Battle of, 173
Cheney, Richard, 26, 28
Chicago Times, 17, 56, 117
Chicago Tribune, 74, 134, 186, 188–89, 206–8

Chickasaw Bayou, 131–44, 146–49, 155, 160, 162, 171. *See also* Vicksburg, Battle of
Christian Commission, U.S., 47, 177, 182
Cincinnati, 52, 87, 95, 176
Cincinnati Commercial, 52, 70, 85, 174; criticism of Sherman by, 74–80; and retraction of insanity charge, 87–88; Sherman sending reporter away, 37–38; and Sherman's treaty, 206–8; support for Sherman by, 92–95, 139, 188–89, 207
Cincinnati Enquirer, 52, 71, 207–8
Cincinnati Gazette, 52, 153, 170, 213; criticism of Sherman at Shiloh, 92, 94; criticism of Sherman by, 75, 121, 134, 179, 207–8; praise for Sherman by, 186; and Sherman insanity charges, 79–80, 135
City Point, Va., 197–99
Civilians, Southern, 112, 183–86
Colburn, Richard T., 141, 158
Constitution, U.S., 12–13, 161–63, 173. *See also* First Amendment
Correspondents. *See* Newsmen
Cronkite, Walter, 29–30
Cumberland, Department of, 66, 70–71, 78
Cumberland Gap, 79, 81
Curtis, Samuel R., 118

Davis, Jefferson, 153–54, 204–6, 208, 214
Democrats, 8, 153
Dix, John A., 17, 204
Douglas, William O., 6

Emancipation Proclamation, 122–23, 183, 215

245

Ewing, Hugh, 42, 153, 179, 213
Ewing, T., Jr., 37–38, 42, 87–88
Ewing, Thomas E., 39–41, 44, 77, 83, 86–88, 153
Ewing family, 39–44, 63–64, 85–88, 93–94, 96–97, 176
Ex Parte Merryman, 33n
Ex Parte Milligan, 13

Falkland Islands War, 22
Fifty-Seventh Article of War, 16–17, 144, 148, 152
First Amendment, 3–5; in the Civil War, 8–15, 17–19, 57–58; discussion of, 224–27; in Knox court-martial, 160–63; Sherman defines, 119–20, 123–24, 126–27, 152–53, 159, 161–63, 171–73; and Supreme Court, 5–9; in wartime, 4–6, 5, 10–12, 15–16
Fort Donelson, 89, 148
Fort Henry, 89, 148
Fort Sumter, 66, 70
Frank Leslie's Illustrated Paper, 80
Fremont, John C., 69, 73

General Orders No. 8, 13th Army Corps, 132, 144, 150–51
General Orders No. 67, 13, 144–45, 147–51, 155
Gentleman's Agreement, 16
Georgia, 46, 187. *See also* Atlanta, march on
Grant, Ulysses S: campaigns of, 89, 178; criticism for Shiloh, 90–91, 93, 95, 96; and Knox court-martial, 147, 150, 152, 157; and Memphis, 109, 112; mentioned, 124, 139, 197; and Sherman, 170–71, 174–76; and Sherman's negotiations with Johnston, 197–204, 210–12; treatment by reporters, 55–56, 93, 95–96; treatment of reporters, 117–18, 160, 187; at Vicksburg, 131–32, 135, 160, 163n, 169–70

Greeley, Horace, 52, 190
Grenada invasion, press in, 10–11, 22–25
"Gulabert," 132

Hackworth, David H., 29
Halleck, Henry W., 56, 108; and Sherman, 170, 186; and Sherman complicity charges, 209–11, 214, 221n; and Sherman insanity charges, 76–78, 81, 85–87
Halstead, Murat, 52, 80–81, 88
Hammond, J. H., 136–37
Hardee, William, 190
Hoffman, Fred, 26
Hood, John Bell, 185–86
House of Representatives, 11
Hudson, Frederic, 50–51
Hurlbut, S. A., 97, 171
Hyman, Harold M., 12, 33n

Indianapolis Journal, 186–87
Isham, Warren P., 117–18, 129n
Ives, Malcolm, 54–55

JB Pictures, Inc. v. United States Department of Defense, 11
Johnston, A. S., 68–69, 102n
Johnston, Joseph E., 198–207, 214, 216
Joint Committee on the Conduct of the War, 211–12
Judiciary Committee, House of Representatives, 15

Keim, De B. Randolph, 179–81, 194n
Kenesaw Mountain, Ga., 185
Kentucky, 177. *See also* Louisville; Muldraugh's Hill; Sherman's command in, 37–38, 66–80, 83, 91–94, 98–99; Sherman's haunted by problems in, 115–16, 125–26, 155, 187, 198
Key, Thomas, 76
Knoll, Erwin, 7

Index

Knox, Thomas W., 110; court-martial of, 141–63, 169, 171; criticism of Sherman, 137–38
Knoxville, Tenn., 174
Korean War, 19–20

Lancaster, Ohio, 38, 41, 78
Lee, Robert E., 178, 199–201, 203, 209
Lee, Stephen D., 163n
Libya, air strikes against, 25
Lincoln, Abraham: assassination of, 200–203, 205–6; and Constitution, 12–13, 225; and Ellen Sherman, 86–87; and Knox court-martial, 141, 156–57, 159; and McClernand, 138, 157; relations with press, 18, 51–52, 54–55, 159; and Sherman, 66, 170, 182, 188–89; and Sherman's agreement with Johnston, 197–206, 208, 211–12; and Sherman's command in Kentucky, 70–71, 86–87, 115; Sherman's mistrust of administration of, 96, 176; Sherman's opinion of, 63, 159, 176; and slavery, 122–23, 182; surrender terms of, 199–204, 208, 211; war strategy of, 97, 197–99
London, England, 42–44, 56
Louisiana, 42–43, 63–64, 83
Louisiana State University, 42–43
Louisville, 37, 69, 72, 73, 79–80, 177
Louisville Journal, 169, 177; on city's neutrality, 67–68; criticism of Sherman in, 134, 206; support for Sherman in, 72, 85, 92, 94, 114, 207–8, 211

McClellan, George B.: Ellen Sherman's opinion of, 87, 115; and General Orders No. 67, 147, 149, 151; and the press, 16, 51; and Sherman's command, 65, 75–76, 78

McClernand, John, 138–41, 157, 159, 163n, 164n
McClure, A. K., 188
McDowell, Irvin, 56
McPherson, James, 179–80
Madison Press Connection, 9
Mail: Sherman's interference with, 134–35, 138; transmitting news reports through, 14–15
March through Carolinas, 190–91, 197–203
March to the sea, 186–89, 196n, 198
Media pools, 24–28
Memphis, Tenn., 132, 160, 171, 198; Sherman in, 99, 108–27
Memphis Appeal, 110–11, 120–21, 135
Memphis *Argus*, 110–11, 120, 160
Memphis *Avalanche*, 110–11
Memphis *Bulletin*, 110, 122–23, 160, 171–73, 179
Memphis *Union Appeal*, 111–13, 118
Meridian, Miss., 174–76, 193n
Metcalf, J., III, 22
Mexican War, 40–41, 64, 83, 98
Military Academy, U.S., 40
Military installations, press access to, 11
Mississippi, 125, 174. *See also* Chickasaw Bayou; Meridian; Vicksburg
Mississippi, Division of, 89, 175
Mississippi River, 109, 131, 160, 168, 174
Missouri: Blairs from, 141, 147; Fremont in, 69, 73; Sherman in, 76–79, 81, 125. *See also* Sedalia; St. Louis
Mitchell, James M., 156
Morton, Charles, 136–37
Muldraugh's Hill, 37, 69–70

Napoleon, 72, 154, 189
The Nation Magazine v. United States Department of Defense, 10–11

National Security. *See* First
    Amendment
Navy, reporters aboard ships,
    56–57
Near v. *Minnesota*, 5–7, 8
Nebraska Press Association v.
    Stuart, 6
New Orleans, 131, 170
New York Associated Press, 51, 72
New York City, 11, 42, 43, 50–52,
    211
New York Commercial Advertiser,
    184
New York Herald, 168, 190;
    criticism of Sherman in, 79,
    117–18; in Knox court-martial,
    150, 154; Knox with, 110,
    137–38, 141; relation with
    military, 53–57; on Sherman,
    114–15, 173, 175–76; on
    Sherman-Johnston agreement,
    205–8; Sherman's attempt to
    control, 159, 180; on Sherman's
    campaigns, 188; status of,
    50–51, 141; support for
    Sherman in, 125, 182, 185–86
New York Journal of Commerce,
    17
New York Times, 57, 156, 182;
    criticism of Sherman in,
    135–36; on Sherman, 78, 186,
    206–8, 213; status of, 51–52;
    support for Sherman in, 70, 72,
    76, 189
New York Tribune, 110, 190, 216;
    and Cameron, 55, 73–74;
    censorship of, 18, 117, 132–33;
    on Knox court-martial, 15456;
    on Sherman, 114–15, 170, 185,
    212; on Sherman-Johnston
    agreement, 206–8; status of,
    51–52
New York World, 17, 141
Newsmen, 51–53 (*see also*
    reporters by name); attitudes
    toward, 21, 53–57, 84, 111;
    commanders' discretion in
    allowing access by, 18, 28;
criticisms of, 29–31, 53, 89–90;
    jailing of, 17, 117–18; and new
    technology, 20–21; registration
    of, 17–18; restrictions on,
    14–18, 22–28, 161–62
Newspapers, 3 (*see also*
    newspapers by name); Civil
    War coverage, 51–54, 56; fear of
    First Amendment rulings, 8, 10;
    not insisting on rights, 27,
    120–21, 191; response to
    restrictions, 28–29, 120–21,
    161–63; Sherman's suppression
    of, 126–27, 161–62, 171–73,
    182; and Sidle Panel, 24–25;
    suppression of, 14, 17, 56–58
North Carolina, 46, 199, 211

Ohio, 38, 41, 92, 96, 153
Ord, Edward, 153

Panama invasion, press in, 25–26
Panic of 1857, 42, 49
Pentagon Papers case, 6–7, 8
Percy, Charles, 9
Persian Gulf War, press in, 10–11,
    29
Philadelphia Inquirer, 169
Pierce v. *U.S.*, 5
Plympton, F. B., 37–38
"Pontiac," 72, 74–75
Poore, Ben Perly, 53
Porter, D. D., 139, 143, 146, 197
Post, T. A., 155
Prentice, G. D., 67, 85, 94, 207
Prior restraint, 6–8, 10, 120
Progressive magazine, 7–10
Public Affairs Officers, 26
Public opinion: influence of press
    on, 4, 21–22; of limitations on
    press, 23–24, 30; military
    manipulation of, 22, 23, 26–28

Raymond, Henry J., 52
Reagan, John A., 200, 201
Reagan, Ronald, 23
Reconstruction, 216
Reid, W. ("Agate"), 79–80, 90–92

Index

Reporters. *See* Newsmen
Republicans, 9, 22n, 51–52, 183, 215
Richardson, A. D., 93, 115, 156, 158
Richmond, 14, 186, 209–10
Roosevelt, Franklin D., 19
Roswell Factory, Ga., 183–84

San Francisco, 42–43, 48–49
San Francisco *Sunday Times*, 48
Sanitary Commission, U.S., 47, 123
Saturday Review, 8
Savannah, Ga., 186, 189, 212
Sawyer, Samuel, 118–19
Schenck v. *U.S.*, 5
Schurz, Carl, 202
Schwartzkopf, Norman, 30
Scott, Thomas, 76
Scott, Winfield, 15–16
Sea Islands order, 215
Sedalia, Mo., 79–80
Seward, William H., 133
Shanks, W. F. G., 176–77
Shepard, Isaac, 147
Sheridan, Phil, 57
Sherman, Ellen E. (wife), 196n, 214; advice to husband, 95, 140, 153; dependence on father, 41, 44, 83; dislike of McClellan, 86, 115; guilt over son's death, 170, 174; marriage of, 41; married life, 44, 83, 124, 176; meeting with Lincoln, 86–87; mentioned, 72, 75; response to insanity charge, 77–78, 86–88, 95; and Shiloh, 96, 124
Sherman, William T., 42; and Admiral Porter, 139–40, 143, 145–46, 197; at Arkansas Post, 139, 141, 148; assumptions about effects of press, 148, 160–61, 190–91; Atlanta campaign of, 177–86, 198; battles with press, 3; and Benjamin Stanton, 96–98, 99; on blacks, 182–83, 215–16; and Blair, 141–43, 147; at Bull Run, 65–66; in California, 41, 42, 48–49; command in Kentucky, 37–38, 66–80, 83, 91–94, 98–99; defense of Grant by, 93, 95–97; depression of, 77–78, 81–82, 86–87, 115–16; description of, 45–48, 82, 109; dislike of politicians, 39–40, 96; early life of, 38–40, 43; and Edwin Stanton, 187, 199, 202–4, 208–9, 211–16, 216, 221n, 222n; and Ewing family, 39–44, 63–64, 78, 85–88, 93–94, 96–97; family life of, 41, 44, 83, 115–16, 170, 174; fear of failure, 47, 63–64, 70–72, 83; fears, 43–44, 75–76; in Grand Review, 212–13; and Grant, 174–76; and Grant at Vicksburg, 131–32, 135, 160, 169–71; and Grant in Knox court-martial, 147, 152; and Grant's relation with press, 117–18, 160; and Halleck, 76–78, 81, 85–87, 108, 170, 186, 209–11, 214, 221n; haunted by command in Kentucky, 115–16, 125–26, 155, 187, 198; in high command meeting, 197–99; history of battles with press, 48–50, 65–66; insanity charges against, 76–88, 104n, 133–36, 206–8; and Jefferson Davis, 153–54, 204–6, 208, 214; John Sherman's advice to, 140, 176, 210–11, 213; John Sherman's support of, 77, 85–88, 93, 154; before Joint Commission on Conduct of War, 211–12; and Knox, 137–38, 141–63; lack of combat in Mexican War, 40–41, 64; and Lincoln, 170, 182, 188–89; and Lincoln's order to Grant, 197–204, 210–12; Lincoln's role in commands of, 66, 70, 71; and Lincoln's surrender terms, 198–204, 208,

Sherman, William T. (*cont.*)
211–12; in Louisiana, 42–43,
63–64; march through
Carolinas by, 190–91, 197–200;
march to the sea by, 186–89,
196n; McClellan's opinion of,
65, 75–76; meeting with
Cameron, 73–74, 73–76;
meeting with Lincoln, 66,
197–98; Meridian Raid by,
174–76, 193n; as military
governor of Memphis, 99–100,
108–29, 130n; in Missouri, 43,
63, 77–79, 81, 86–87;
motivation for battles with
press, 48, 58, 98–99, 123–24,
126–27, 143–44; opinion of
Civil War, 43, 47–48; opinion of
Federal forces, 63–65, 126;
opinion of Lincoln, 63–64, 96,
115, 176; opinion of
McClernand, 157, 159;
promotions of, 70, 95, 170–71,
175–76; and Reid, 79, 91–92;
replacement by McClernand,
138–40, 164n; response to
Emancipation Proclamation,
122–23, 183, 215; at Shiloh,
89–99, 116, 124; and slavery, 40,
121–23, 182–83, 214; soldiers'
feelings for, 46, 124; surrender
agreement with Johnston,
198–207, 214, 216–18; and U.S.
Christian Commission, 47, 177,
182; and U.S. Sanitary
Commission, 47, 123; at
Vicksburg, 125, 131–44,
146–47, 155, 160, 162, 168–71;
and Villard, 72, 80–81, 93, 173
Shiloh, Battle of: criticism of
Union generals at, 55, 89–91,
93, 96–99, 106n; Ewings's
letters on, 93–95; news
coverage of, 89–97; praise for
Sherman at, 91–93; restores
Sherman, 92–93, 116, 124, 127,
198
Sidle, Winant, 24, 26

Sidle Panel, 24–26
Slaves, 41, 121–23, 182–83, 211,
215–16. *See also* Blacks
Smith, Elias, 205–6
Somalia, newsmen in, 30–31
Spanish-American War, 19
"Specials." *See* Newsmen
Spooner, John A., 182–83
St. Louis, 42, 66, 79, 149;
Sherman in, 43, 63, 76–78
St. Louis Missouri Democrat, 114,
117, 121–22, 134, 153
St. Louis Missouri Republican,
134, 147, 154, 206–8
Stanton, Benjamin, 96–99
Stanton, Edwin M., 18, 54–55,
187, 199, 202–4, 208–9, 211–16,
221n, 222n
Steele, Frederick, 147
Stevens, Thaddeus, 12
Sumner, Charles, 12
Supreme Court, on First
Amendment issues, 5–7, 11–12,
227

Taney, Roger B., 20n
Telegraphs: censorship of
newsreports on, 14–15, 19, 55;
dependence of newspapers on,
51
Tennessee, 69, 75, 86, 108–27,
174
Thayer, John M., 144, 157, 159
Thomas, George A., 180–81
Thomas, Lorenzo, 73–74

*U.S. ex rel Milwaukee Democrat
Publishing Co.* v. *Burleson*, 5

Van Renasselaer, C., 144–46,
150–52
Vessey, John W., Jr., 24
Vicksburg, Battle of, 125, 131–44,
146–49, 155, 159, 160, 162,
168–69. *See also* Chickasaw
Bayou
Vietnam War, 6, 162; censorship
in, 19–21

Villard, H., 72, 80–81, 93, 173
Virginia, 178, 203

Wallace, Lew, 110, 118
War Department, 10, 14, 64, 70, 148, 187, 204
Warren, Robert, 7–8
Washington, D.C., 14; administration's response to Sherman, 75–76, 81, 201–2; Ellen Sherman in, 86–88; Grand Review in, 212–13; Sherman in, 63–64, 66–67
Washington Chronicle, 154, 186, 206–8
Washington Post, 8, 27
Washington Republican, 185
Washington Star, 114, 206–8

Webb, William E., 147, 154
Weinberger, Casper, 23
West Tennessee, District of, 124
Western Associated Press, 51
Whig Party, 39
Wilkeson, Samuel, 55, 73–74, 80
Wilkie, Franc B., 53–54, 135–37, 141
Williams, George R., 57
Williams, Pete, 26, 29
Woods, W. B., 145–47, 149–50
World War I, 4–5, 162; voluntary censorship in, 16, 19
World War II, 21; voluntary censorship in, 16, 19
Worthington, Thomas, 106n

Young's Point, La., 144